Let's Make Bitters!

to the
Sweetest Man

♡

Quarto is the authority on a wide range of topics.

Quarto educates, entertains and enriches the lives of our readers—enthusiasts and lovers of hands-on living.

www.quartoknows.com

© 2016 Quarto Publishing Group USA Inc.
Text © 2016 Erin Coopey

First published in 2016 by Cool Springs Press,
an imprint of Quarto Publishing Group USA Inc.,
400 First Avenue North, Suite 400, Minneapolis, MN 55401 USA.
Telephone: (612) 344-8100 Fax: (612) 344-8692

quartoknows.com
Visit our blogs at quartoknows.com

Cool Springs Press titles are also available at discounts in bulk quantity for industrial or sales-promotional use. For details contact the Special Sales Manager at Quarto Publishing Group USA Inc., 400 First Avenue North, Suite 400, Minneapolis, MN 55401 USA.

10 9 8 7 6 5 4 3 2 1

ISBN: 978-1-59186-654-1

Library of Congress Cataloging-in-Publication Data

Names: Coopey, Erin, author.
Title: Infusing flavors / Erin Coopey.
Description: Minneapolis, MN : Cool Springs Press, 2016.
Identifiers: LCCN 2015047474 | ISBN 9781591866541 (paperback)
Subjects: LCSH: Cooking (Spices) | Herbal teas. | Flavoring essences. |
   Essences and essential oils. | Non-alcoholic beverages—Flavor and odor. |
   Oils and fats—Flavor and odor. | BISAC: COOKING / Beverages / General. |
   COOKING / Methods / General. | COOKING / Specific Ingredients / Herbs,
   Spices, Condiments. | LCGFT: Cookbooks.
Classification: LCC TX819.A1 C6548 2016 | DDC 641.6/383--dc23
LC record available at http://lccn.loc.gov/2015047474

Acquiring Editor: Billie Brownell
Project Managers: Alyssa Bluhm and Caitlin Fultz
Art Direction and Cover Design: Cindy Samargia Laun
Book Design and Layout: Amy Sly
Photography (unless noted below): Paul Markert (markertproductions.com) and Dave Bausman (tilt-photo.com)
   Erin Coopey: 79, 102. Shutterstock: 1, 4, 9, 11 (left top and bottom), 13, 17, 19, 20, 21, 22, 24, 25,
   26, 27, 29, 33, 35, 36, 40, 55, 60, 62, 72, 75, 80, 83, 88, 97, 104, 111, 120, 125, 136, 154, 156, 169
Food Stylist: Maggie Stopera (maggiethefoodstylist.com)

Printed in China

INTENSE INFUSIONS FOR FOOD AND DRINK

INFUSING
FLAVORS

Recipes for oils, vinegars, sauces, bitters, waters & more

ERIN COOPEY

COOL
SPRINGS
PRESS
Home and Garden Experts™

MINNEAPOLIS, MINNESOTA

Dedication

For Vince: Love, laughs, lust, and life. —Erin

Acknowledgments

This book started in a surprising way. I received a phone call from my now-editor, Billie Brownell, with an intriguing idea for a book. Our conversation revealed that the idea had blossomed from beverages to an entire world of infusions. Billie's vision sparked a flurry of brainstorming. Together, we quickly came up with the framework for what would become the book you are reading today. It's been a thrilling process, and I am grateful to Billie and the other staff at Cool Springs Press for entrusting it to me.

Thank you to my friends and neighbors who graciously tasted various versions of recipes I tested: Jen and Caitlyn, Debi, David, Kristi and Tim, Glenn, Sarah and Rick, Kelli and Elise, and Natasha. I also want to thank all of my friends, students, and assistants who tested recipes for me: Michael B., Carol R., Jessica S., June C., Cathy S., Claire P., Leigh P., Barbara E., Nancy H., Jan B., Sylvia K., Skip D., Leslie C., Jen S., Maria C., and Shelly J. Your input was invaluable and so appreciated.

A special thank-you to my mother, novelist Judith Redline Coopey. By her own admission, she's not all that interested in cooking, but I rely on her sharp editorial eye and her "everyday cook" questions. She makes sure my recipes read well and that I'm not writing in chef-speak.

Thanks also to my dear husband, Vince Harrelson—my number-one tester and gentle critic. You always balance critical insight and constructive feedback with kindness and tact. I couldn't ask for a better sounding board. Thank you for all your love, support, and patience.

Finally, I say a huge thank-you to you for choosing to read *Infusing Flavors*. If you enjoyed it, I would be very grateful if you could write a review. I'd love to hear what you think, and reviews really help people discover my cookbooks.

Contents

The Flavor Revolution

IT SEEMS AS THOUGH EVERYWHERE YOU TURN THESE DAYS, people are talking about infusions. There are infused oils and vinegars for salads and infused broths to transform everyday soups and sauces into exotic creations. The beverage industry is awash with infused waters and juices. Infused alcohols run the gamut from whipped cream to bacon flavor. Cocktails are doctored with bitters and simple syrups (both infusions in their own right), and don't even get me started on desserts. It's like we're all mad scientists toiling in our kitchen laboratories creating Frank-infusions.

We may be in the middle of an infusion revolution, but the idea of infusion dates back to the dawn of cooking. Who knows who first broke off a fragrant flower or leaf and added it to hot water? Or who accidentally dropped some garlic into oil only to discover that one pleasantly enhanced the other?

In the most traditional sense, an infusion is the creation of a new substance by steeping or soaking botanicals in a liquid such as water, vinegar, oil, or alcohol. These days the term is even broadly used to describe the addition of flavors to a dish, such as bourbon-infused barbecue sauce.

I've always been interested in making things from scratch, so infusions are a natural progression in my growth as a chef. In this book we'll explore a variety of infusions—from teas and tisanes to extracts, broths, vinegars, oils, desserts, and more. If you're captivated by the creativity of cooking and combining flavors, infusing is for you.

Viva el infusión!

Creating: Getting Started Infusing Flavors

For me, creating infusions occurs organically. I get a spark, an inspiration, from something I see or taste. Suddenly my internal Rolodex (yes, I'm old school) begins to whirl. Where have I tasted this before? What does it remind me of? What goes with it? From then on, it's about experimenting.

I'm not an herbalist. I approach infusions from a cook's perspective—what tastes good together? Why not mix mint with basil? They're cousins after all. Would pineapple go with rosemary? Let's see! Infusions spark our imaginations—inducing us to take something standard, reimagine it, and make it our own.

I want to give you two pieces of advice for creating new infusions: trust your instincts, and be open to experimenting. Don't be afraid to try what pops into your mind, to deviate from the infusion, just for fun. For me that's the beauty of cooking: it lets you tap into your creative side.

You can find inspiration almost anywhere—in your garden, spice rack, or market. Taste. Adjust. Taste again. If the flavor isn't quite right, try something else. It's all about experimenting. You may discover an innovative infusionist hiding in your cook's brain.

Blending: Experimenting with Flavors

When it comes to blending, balance is essential. An infusion should be a pleasant marriage of flavors. One element should never dominate so much that it's all you experience. Think of infusions as layers of a parfait, each layer building on another to create something more interesting than the individual ingredients alone.

Blending can bring together opposing flavors—sweet and salty like salted caramel, or sweet and sour like lemon drops, or bitter and sweet like dark chocolate. Or we can find balance blending complementary flavors such as rosemary and thyme, or vanilla and cream. You probably already have combinations that you like together, so that's a great place to start.

Health Benefits

Although most of us know that fruits and vegetables are "good for us," we don't have a deep understanding of the health benefits of botanicals. For example, did you know that cherries contain substances that fight inflammation? Or that an ounce of watercress has as much vitamin C as an orange?

The same goes for herbs and spices. Not only do they improve the taste of foods, but they can have antibacterial and antiviral properties. Certainly herbs are better known for their homeopathic uses, but most of us don't think, "Wow, this headache is killing me. Better eat some basil!"

As I mentioned, I am not an herbalist, but I do find learning about herbs and their properties fascinating. I also believe firmly in the health benefits of making food and drinks from scratch. Being able to choose what goes into your food is empowering. I'd much rather sip a soda made from real vanilla syrup than imitation vanilla flavor, wouldn't you? (Incidentally, ancient Mayans believed that vanilla had aphrodisiacal properties, but we haven't been able to prove that scientifically. Darn!) So, throughout this book, I've included notes about commonly accepted health benefits and interesting tidbits about some of the ingredients.

Brewing & Infusing

I used several techniques in the book, including standard infusing, cold infusing, and decocting. The technique you choose depends largely on what you are trying to extract flavor from.

A **Standard infusing** is basically steeping, like making tea. It's the most common way to infuse the flavors of herbs and flowers into water.

B **Cold infusing** is a slower process that relies on time to extract flavor. It's how you make infused vinegars, extracts, and bitters.

C **Decocting** is simmering. It's used to bring out the flavors from more dense materials such as roots, rhizomes, and barks. Teas and tisanes made from ginger and turmeric rely on decocting. It's also used to infuse broths and cream.

D **Percolating** is the act of infusing by running liquid through permeable substances. Think coffee. I thought it might be fun to include a Percolator Punch (page 89).

Equipment

The nicest thing about infusions is that they don't require any high-tech gadgets. There are a few items, however, that I find helpful to have on hand.

Nonreactive Bowls & Pans
Have you ever cooked tomato sauce in cast iron or an old aluminum pan? Did you notice a metallic taste? That's the reaction between acidic foods and a "reactive" pan, which we are trying to avoid by choosing nonreactive materials. Glass, pyroceramic glass, ceramic, or stainless steel bowls and pans don't react to acidic ingredients such as vinegar or tomatoes. Nonreactive bowls and pans are essential to successful infusions—particularly when you're making shrubs, vinegars, and some broths.

Muslin Spice Bags or Tea Sachets

I use small muslin spice bags from my local Chinese herbalist to add spices and barks for some of the bitters. Tea sachets work well too, so I always have a few of each on hand. Both are liquid permeable and allow you to control the strength of flavors during the infusions. If you throw all your ingredients in at one time, you can't finesse taste.

Cheesecloth can be used to strain or to steep.

Wide-Mouth Mason Jars

Available at most grocery stores and a few old-fashioned hardware stores, Mason jars are inexpensive and versatile. Wide mouths make them easy to fill and to empty. I use all sizes from ¼ pint to 1 gallon. In fact, they are so ubiquitous in our house that my husband and I use them for drinking glasses too.

Crocks

A good old-fashioned earthenware crock isn't essential, but I get quite a bit of use out of mine.

I have two sizes—quart and gallon. The gallon-size gets the most use—from cooling Old-Fashioned Root Beer to making Homemade Apple Cider Vinegar to fermenting kombucha. And, there is *nothing* like crock-fermented sauerkraut; check out my other book, *The Kitchen Pantry Cookbook* (Quarry Books), if you want to learn how.

Cheesecloth

I can't tell you how much cheesecloth I've gone through writing this book. When a sieve isn't fine enough, cheesecloth is your best friend. It's so simple to use: You simply cut it to size and you can make the mesh as fine as you wish by adding multiple layers. You can choose whether to purchase the natural or bleached variety.

Funnels

Funnels of all shapes and sizes—from the wide canning variety to tiny tapered flask size—I use them all. Canning funnels are useful anytime you are filling Mason jars. As much as I try to take my time, use a steady hand, and aim carefully, I still spill sometimes, so a good canning funnel is an essential for me. Standard tapered funnels in various sizes will help you package and store all the extracts, bitters, oils, and vinegars you make.

Fine-Mesh Sieves

It seems like I am always reaching into the cupboard for a sieve. I have sizes ranging from individual tea strainer to large saucepan-width. I also have a vintage China cap (a conical sieve, also called a *chinois*) on a stand with a wooden pestle, which I *love*. Almost every infusion you make will be strained at some point in the process. You don't have to go crazy and get yourself a chinois, but I do recommend a set of three or so sieves in various sizes. Be sure that you choose sieves with stainless steel mesh so they are nonreactive with acidic ingredients.

Masking Tape & Fine-Tipped Marker

If you have also read *The Kitchen Pantry Cookbook*, you may already know that masking tape is an essential in my kitchen. I'd be surrounded by mystery jars without it. I identify all my infusions by name and date. It's particularly helpful during the infusion process, but it's also useful for storage. Sometimes after you've made several infusions, they all begin to look alike. In addition, contrary to what we might wish, nothing lasts forever. You may think you'll never forget the day you made that *fantastic* Pizza Drizzle Oil, but what happens when you find it in the back of the refrigerator later? Was that July or August? Is it still good? I don't know about you, but sometimes I need a little reminder. Write a label. You'll thank me later.

Dark-Tinted Tincture Bottles

I purchase small, 4-ounce amber glass bottles with built-in droppers from Glass Bottle Outlet (see Resources). They are great for storing both extracts and bitters. The dark color protects your infusion from damaging UV rays and light degradation. You can choose among amber, cobalt blue, and green in various sizes, caps, and dispensers. They make lovely gifts too. Just add a pretty label!

Labels

My handwriting is terrible, though I was once told it would be perfect for a comic strip! If I'm planning to give away any of my infusions as gifts, I always create a label. (I'm not saying your handwriting is as bad as mine, but penmanship, not to mention calligraphy, seems to be a dying art.) Thank goodness, Avery has developed a whole line of pretty specialty labels and tags—including some Martha Stewart designs for the aspiring perfectionist in all of us. Since most of us have printers at home, it's pretty easy to create a label that reflects all the care you put into your infusion.

Infusion Carafes and Pitchers

If you like infused waters, you might want to splurge on an infusion carafe or pitcher from Prodyne (or another supplier; see Resources). I have several and find them to be both pretty and functional. Not only can you add fresh water to existing ingredients to stretch your infusions but they are easy to clean and make serving simple.

Storing

Each infusion has different storage requirements. Some are naturally shelf stable, while others require refrigeration. For example, alcohol and vinegar are naturally resistant to bacterial growth, while broths and oils are more susceptible. Some infusions can be stored for months, while others should be used in a matter of days. That's the nature of do-it-yourself foods; sometimes we have to sacrifice longevity for natural ingredients, so each chapter includes information on storing.

One piece of advice I've repeated throughout the book regards sterilization. You should *always* store your infusions in clean, sterilized containers. Even if you plan to use them in a matter of days, storing them in sterilized bottles and jars will help to ensure safety. With oil in particular, the container must be sterile and completely dry. Water residue can lead to bacterial growth.

How to Sterilize Bottles, Jars & Containers

Although there are many ways to sterilize containers—from dry heat to chemical—the most reliable method is boiling. Here's a step-by-step guide:

- Wash your bottles and jars in hot soapy water and rinse thoroughly. Be sure that your containers are free of debris and detergent.

- Place the clean containers in a large pot. Fill the pot with hot water. Make sure that the water covers and fills the containers, covering the bottles and jars by at least 1 inch.

- Bring the water to a boil over high heat.

- Set a timer, and boil for 10 minutes. If you live at a high elevation, add 1 minute of boiling time for every 1,000 feet of elevation over 1,000 feet. For example, if you live in Denver, elevation 5,000 feet, you would boil your containers for 14 minutes. That's 10 minutes for the first 1,000 feet, and 1 additional minute for every 1,000 feet above that (4,000 feet equals 4 minutes).

- Turn off the heat. Using tongs or jar lifters, remove the containers from the pot and carefully pour out the water.

- Place the containers on a clean kitchen towel. If you're adding infusions made with vinegar or alcohol, you may fill the containers while they are still warm. If you're adding an oil-based infusion, allow the container to air dry completely.

Okay, now that you've got the basics, let's start infusing flavors!

Sterilizing jars in boiling water will ensure safe storage.

Teas & Tisanes

1

YOU'VE ALREADY TRIED YOUR HAND AT INFUSING and didn't even realize it. The simple act of steeping a teabag in hot water is the basis for infusing. You're practically an expert! Teas and tisanes are the oldest form of infusion. Mankind discovered fire, and not long after we sat down with a cup of tea to talk about it.

We use the word "tea" to describe most herbal beverages, whether they are made with tea leaves or herbs and flowers, but it's more accurate to describe herbal infusions as *tisanes*. Tisane is a French word meaning "herbal infusion."

Tisanes were originally medicinal blends made from herbs, flowers, roots, barks, and fruits. These days, tisanes, or herbal teas, are primarily enjoyed for their flavor and lack of caffeine.

Cheers to Good Health!

Tisanes can be made with both fresh and dried flowers and herbs, in addition to leaves, whole spices, seeds, roots, and barks. Infusions are made by steeping the flowers or herbs in very hot water (just under boiling), 5 to 7 minutes as a general guideline. Remember, whole spices, seeds, roots, and barks, on the other hand, need to be simmered (decocted) to extract their flavor and medicinal elements. You may need to decoct a root for as long as 15 minutes.

When making your own tisane with dried herbs and flowers, a common ratio is 1 ounce of herbs to 8 ounces of water. If you are using fresh herbs, try a small handful for every 8 ounces of water.

Here are some of the more common herbs, flowers, spices, and roots used in tisanes, along with their reputed benefits.

Anise: Anise is used to treat asthma, colds and coughs, sore throats, and bad breath. Both the seeds and leaves are used to flavor teas.

Bee Balm or Wild Bergamot: When brewed in Colonial times, it was called Oswego tea. A member of the mint family, bee balm was used for relief from fever, nausea, headaches, and sore throat.

Caraway Seeds: Caraway seeds are used for treating stomach and digestive issues including heartburn, bloating, gas, mild stomachache, and loss of appetite.

Catnip: Not just for kitty! Catnip is used for treating insomnia, anxiety, and migraine headaches, as well as respiratory issues.

Chamomile: Chamomile is used for soothing anxiety and stomach upset.

Cinnamon: Cinnamon is used to treat inflammation.

Citrus peel, including Bergamot, Lemon, and Orange (particularly bitter orange such as bergamot): These citrus components are believed to relieve abdominal distention and chest congestion.

Cloves (clove oil and buds): Clove oil has been used to treat toothache. Cloves also contain anesthetic and antibacterial properties.

Dandelion: High in Vitamins C and B complex, dandelion is also mildly diuretic and can improve liver and kidney functions.

Dill: A good source of calcium, dill is used in the treatment of everything from insomnia to menstrual symptoms.

Echinacea: Echinacea is used to boost the immune system and support the respiratory system against colds and flu.

Elderberry: Noted for its antioxidants, elderberry is also thought to lower cholesterol and boost the immune system against coughs, colds, and flu.

Fennel: Containing iron, calcium, magnesium, and other minerals, fennel is also consumed for bone health and may lower blood pressure.

Ginger Root: Long thought of as a digestive aid, ginger root is used to reduce inflammation in the colon and to help control nausea. In addition, scientific studies on ginger have shown benefits for many ailments ranging from asthma to menstrual pain.

Ginseng: Ginseng is thought to boost the immune system as well as lower blood sugar and improve concentration and mood.

Hibiscus: Hibiscus has a gentle laxative effect and is used to treat high blood pressure. It may also improve appetite and settle the stomach.

Lemon Balm: Lemon balm is used for a variety of digestive complaints, including upset stomach, bloating, gas, and vomiting. Lemon balm is also believed to have calming effects, so it's used for treating anxiety, ADHD, and sleep disorders.

Lemongrass: The main component of lemongrass, lemonal, has antibacterial and antimicrobial properties. It is used for treating a multitude of health problems ranging from high cholesterol to infections. In Ayurvedic medicine, lemongrass is used to lower fevers.

Licorice Root: Licorice root is used as an anti-inflammatory; overuse can increase blood pressure, however, so don't go overboard.

Mint: One of the most popular digestive aids, peppermint is good for everything from stomachaches, stomach pains, and stomach cramps to diarrhea.

Nettle Leaf: A natural antihistamine, nettle leaves are also good for stomach ailments.

Chamomile tea has long been used to treat anxiety. You can use fresh or dried flowers.

Red Raspberry Leaf: Has as anti-inflammatory compounds, so red raspberry leaves are used in the treatment of gout, arthritis, and other inflammatory ailments.

Rose Hips: High in vitamin C and great for preventing bladder infections, rose hips can also be helpful for easing headaches and dizziness.

Rosemary: Long thought to improve memory, rosemary turns out to contain an ingredient that fights off free radicals that might damage the brain. Rosemary was traditionally used to help alleviate muscle pain,

improve memory, boost the immune and circulatory systems, and promote hair growth.

Sage: While the oils and tannins have astringent and antiseptic properties that make them helpful in treating mouth sores and sore throats, tea from sage leaves is reputed to relieve flatulence and aid digestion.

Stevia: Although stevia has become quite popular as a sugar alternative, medicinally it has been used for obesity, hypertension, and heartburn and to help lower uric acid levels.

Fresh Mint Tisane

Mint tisanes date back to ancient Greece, where mint symbolized hospitality. I like this tea with Ginger-Infused Honey (page 154). SERVES 4 TO 6

6 cups water

1 cup packed fresh mint leaves

Sugar or honey, to taste, optional

Mint sprigs for garnish, optional

Fill a ceramic teapot with hot tap water to preheat it, and let sit while you bring 6 cups of water to just under a boil in a saucepan or teakettle.

Empty the teapot of the tap water. Place the mint leaves in the bottom of the teapot. Carefully pour in the boiling water. Stir once to combine.

Let steep for 5 to 10 minutes. Pour the tisane through a strainer into individual cups. You may want to stop and swirl the pot from time to time so the leaves don't clog the spout.

Sweeten with sugar or honey, if desired. Garnish with fresh mint sprigs.

Mint "Jam"—Riffing on the Differences between Spearmint and Peppermint

The two most common mint varieties are peppermint and spearmint, but what's the difference? **Spearmint**, a native of Europe, is referred to as common mint, garden mint, Our Lady's mint, and sage of Bethlehem. The leaves are long, spear shaped, and attach to the stalk of the plant versus the stems. Spearmint is most commonly used in teas, mint juleps, mojitos, candy, and gum. **Peppermint** is a hybrid of spearmint. It's also been called American mint, lamb mint (or lam-mint). It was native to Europe and brought to America by the colonists. The leaves are 1 to 2 inches long and have a toothed edge. Peppermint is used in tea and for flavoring ice cream, candy, gum, and toothpaste.

Although they both come from the *Mentha* plant genus, peppermint contains more menthol so it may seem stronger. Spearmint is sometimes described as greener or sweeter, while peppermint has a candy cane flavor. I don't think you can go wrong with either. It's just a matter of personal preference.

Both varieties are easy to grow. They thrive in moist, part-sun to shady locations, and spread quickly by underground rhizomes or runners (these are sneaky little shoots that pop up in seemingly random places). I planted some mint in a container full of various herbs thinking, novice gardener that I am, I could control the stuff with pruning. *Wrong!* I learned quickly that there is no use struggling with it, because *it will take over*. So I suggest if you plant mint, give it its own pot, and don't plant it in your open garden.

Fresh Nettle Tisane

Nettle leaves contain antihistamine and anti-inflammatory properties. Many people, myself included, drink nettle tisane to combat springtime allergies. SERVES 2

2 cups water

2 large handfuls fresh nettle leaves (collected with a gloved hand)

Honey, to sweeten, if desired

Place the water in a saucepan or kettle. Bring to a boil. While you are waiting, fill a ceramic teapot with hot tap water to preheat it.

When the water is just under a boil, empty your preheated teapot. Carefully toss in the nettle leaves and pour the boiling water over the leaves. Cover and allow to steep for 10 minutes.

Alternatively, you can simply add the nettle leaves to the saucepan of boiling water. Remove the pan from the heat. Cover and allow to steep for 10 minutes. This is sometimes easier than pushing the nettle leaves into a teapot.

Strain nettle tisane into two mugs. Sweeten with honey to taste and enjoy.

How to Harvest Stinging Nettles

Growing up in rural Wisconsin, I became well acquainted with stinging nettles. My brother and I were sure to come home with welts after playing in the woods or along the creek.

Stinging nettles first appear in early spring. The plants can get as tall as 6 feet. Their leaves are heart shaped with toothed edges. The stems and leaves have tiny hollow spines. If pricked, the spines lodge in your skin and release formic acid, among other things, which causes welts.

I suggest that you bring along work gloves, scissors, and a basket to carry the leaves when harvesting nettles. It's also a good idea to wear long sleeves and long pants so that you aren't stung while brushing past the plants.

As with any wild plant, you should be certain that they haven't been sprayed with pesticides.

Harvest the top bud and upper leaves of the plants; they tend to be most tender. In addition, taking the top bud encourages the plant to grow more bushy side sprouts, which ensures there will be more buds to harvest later. Nettles continue to grow through the fall, though most people recommend picking them before they flower and go to seed.

Once you bring the leaves home, rinse them under cold running water to wash away any debris. Use a colander and tongs or gloves to rinse them. Remember, they can still sting you. Cooking the nettles takes the sting out, so once you boil them they become harmless.

Fresh-picked nettles can be stored in baggies in the refrigerator for two to three days, or they can be dried for later use. The dehydration process does make them easier to handle, but there's still a chance of irritation. To dry, either hang bundles of leafy stems in a dry location, or place the leaves in a food dehydrator.

Nettles can be eaten as well as made into tisane. Cooked nettles can be substituted for spinach in many recipes. You can simply sauté in a little butter or oil and season with salt and pepper. You can also make **nettle vinegar** by steeping dried or fresh leaves in apple cider vinegar for 3 to 6 weeks.

Chamomile-Lavender Tisane

Lavender and chamomile combine to make this relaxing tisane. It's lovely just before bedtime. SERVES 2

2 cups water

6 tablespoons fresh chamomile flowers, or 3 tablespoons dried

2 teaspoons dried culinary lavender flowers, or 3½ to 4 teaspoons fresh lavender buds

Place the water in a kettle and bring to just under a boil. While you are waiting, fill a teapot with hot tap water to preheat it.

When the water in the kettle is hot, empty your preheated teapot and add the chamomile and lavender. Pour the hot water over them. Allow to steep for about 10 minutes. Strain through a tea strainer and enjoy.

You might also like to add a twist of lemon and a little honey to your tea.

Erin's Tip: In general, when I make tea from loose tea leaves or dried herbs and flowers, I like to put them directly into the water as opposed to a tea ball or enclosed strainer. I feel the flavors are deeper if the leaves and flowers can move freely in the water. When the tea has steeped, I pour it into my cup through a fine tea strainer. If you prefer, however, you can substitute a tea ball.

Cooking with Lavender

Most varieties of lavender can be used for cooking, but you do need to be sure that they have not been treated with pesticides. Though it thrives outdoors in sunny well-drained soil, lavender can also be grown indoors. English lavender (*L. angustifolia* 'Munstead') has the sweetest fragrance, which makes it the best suited for cooking. The blossoms can also be used in salads, baked goods, roasted meats—particularly lamb—and creamy desserts, but, remember, a little goes a long way!

Tarragon-Berry Tisane

Placing tarragon in a traveler's shoe was once thought to provide stamina and endurance. I don't know about that, but this tisane sure is refreshing! SERVES 4

4 cups water

2 tablespoons fresh tarragon leaves

1 cup raspberries

Honey, to taste, optional

Measure the water into a teakettle or saucepan. Bring to just under a boil over high heat.

While you are waiting for the water to heat, place the fresh tarragon leaves and raspberries in a teapot or spouted bowl. Using a wooden spoon or cocktail muddler, bruise the leaves and crush the berries.

Pour the hot water over the crushed leaves and berries and steep for 10 minutes.

Pour the tisane through a fine-mesh strainer into teacups. Sweeten with honey, if using.

Erin's Tip: Try this tisane over ice or make it like an infused water—add the water, bruised tarragon leaves, and raspberries to an infusion pitcher. Refrigerate overnight and enjoy. You should be able to refill your infusion pitcher once or twice and still get great flavored water.

Turmeric Tisane

Although ground turmeric may be easier to purchase, the drying process does diminish some of its essential oils and, hence, its pungency. If you have access to fresh turmeric, it's *definitely* the way to go, and you'll find the flavor is much richer. SERVES 4

4 cups water

1 teaspoon grated fresh turmeric, or ½ teaspoon ground turmeric

1 teaspoon peeled and grated fresh ginger, or pinch ground ginger

Pinch cayenne pepper, optional

1 tablespoon freshly squeezed lemon juice

1 to 2 tablespoons maple syrup or honey, to taste, optional

Pour the water into a medium saucepan. Add the turmeric, ginger, and cayenne. If you are using powdered spices, be sure to whisk until blended. Slowly bring to a simmer over medium heat. Simmer for 10 minutes.

Remove from the heat. Stir in the lemon juice. Strain the tisane into mugs and add the maple syrup or honey, if using.

If you are using powdered spices, you should stir your tea between sips so that the spices don't settle to the bottom.

Turmeric

Turmeric is a cousin of ginger. In fact, you might have confused it with ginger in the grocery store. It shares that same knobby look, though it's generally smaller than ginger. Under its thin skin you'll find that trademark yellow-orange color. Fresh turmeric has an earthy, peppery flavor. It's been getting more attention lately because it contains a chemical called "curcumin," reputed to reduce inflammation.

You can typically find fresh turmeric in grocery stores specializing in Asian or Indian food. It is also carried in many gourmet markets and health food stores. Always select firm rhizomes (sometimes called roots).

Earl Grey Tea

You can also add bergamot oil to loose-leaf black tea to make your own Earl Grey.
Black tea is typically used, but the type you choose is up to you. I like Ceylon or
any other black tea with lightly floral notes.

**20 to 30 drops bergamot oil
(see Bergamot Buyer Beware)**

**8 ounces good-quality black
loose-leaf tea**

**2 to 3 tablespoons dried orange peel
(bitter or sweet, your choice), optional**

Put 20 to 30 drops of bergamot oil on a couple of clean cotton balls or a small piece of paper towel. Place in the bottom of a Mason jar or another airtight container.

Add tea and the dried orange peel, if using, to the jar. Close the lid tightly, and shake the jar to blend.

Let the tea sit for at least 48 hours to infuse with the oil. I like strong bergamot flavor, so I usually leave the cotton balls in the tea leaves for 1 to 2 weeks.

To see if it's finished, brew a cup of tea. If you like the flavor, it's done! You can remove the cotton balls when you are happy with the flavor. Keep the jar closed tightly when stored so that the bergamot oil doesn't evaporate and lose its citrus punch.

Bergamot Buyer Beware

When buying bergamot oil, always read the label to be sure that you are purchasing *Citrus bergamia* or *Citrus aurantium* made from bergamot citrus peel. The label should state that it can be used in food or that it's food grade. It's also a good idea to purchase organic bergamot oil. Bergamot oil is extracted from the peel, and nonorganic might mean that the oranges were sprayed or otherwise chemically treated.

There's an herb called bergamot (also called bee balm and wild bergamot). Bee balm has a sharp, citrusy, slightly minty nose when it's crushed, but if you're looking for the real deal for your tea, go with bergamot oil instead.

Peppermint Green Tea with Bergamot Oil

This light citrus-mint combo is great hot or iced. SERVES 4

4 cups water

½ cup packed fresh mint leaves

3 bags of your favorite green tea (for iced tea, double the number of teabags)

1 to 2 drops bergamot oil

Honey, to taste, optional

Fill a ceramic teapot with hot tap water to preheat it, and set aside while you heat the water for tea.

Bring the water to just under a boil in a kettle.

Empty the teapot and add the mint leaves. Using a wooden spoon or cocktail muddler, crush the leaves slightly to release the oils.

Pour the hot water over the mint leaves and steep for 5 to 10 minutes. (I like to steep the mint for 10 minutes if I'm making iced tea.)

Add the green tea and steep for 2 to 3 minutes longer.

Stir in the bergamot oil; add honey, if using, and serve.

Erin's Tip: Bergamot oil is very strong, so experiment with how you add it. I suggest using a dropper from a tincture bottle so you can control the amount. You can also add a tiny amount by dipping a toothpick into the oil and then swirling the toothpick in your tea.

Orange-Clove Tea

Black tea with orange is one of my favorite comforts. SERVES 2

2 cups water

3 teaspoons loose-leaf (or 2 teabags) black tea

1 orange, cut into ¼-inch-thick slices

10 whole cloves, divided

Honey or sugar, if desired

Fill a ceramic teapot with hot tap water to preheat it.

Place 2 cups of water in a kettle or pan. Heat the kettle over high heat.

When the water is just under a boil, empty your teapot and add 5 or 6 orange slices, 6 cloves, and the tea. (I like to let my tea float freely in my teapot, but you can use a tea ball or infuser if you prefer.) Fill the teapot with hot water from the kettle. Let steep for 3 to 5 minutes.

While the tea is infusing, place a slice of orange and a clove or two into each teacup.

Strain the tea through a fine strainer into the orange-filled cup. Add sweetener, if using, and serve.

Tea Time! Brewing Basics

Optimum brewing temperatures and times vary from tea to tea but here are some general brewing guidelines:

Don't overheat the water. Boiling can evaporate the essential oils that produce the flavor in both teas and tisanes.

Preheat for consistency. No matter what tea you plan to enjoy, it's always a good idea to preheat your cup or pot with hot water before you start to brew your tea. It helps to keep the water temperature consistent.

Filtered water will ensure better-tasting tea. Using a quality sand or charcoal filter (such as a Brita) for tap water can remove a metallic taste or off flavors.

Ginger & Raspberry Infusion

3 tablespoons peeled and minced ginger
(about a 2-inch chunk of fresh ginger)

1 cup raspberries, fresh or frozen

4 cups water

Measure 3 tablespoons of minced ginger into a saucepan. Add the raspberries and water. Bring to just under a boil. Turn off heat, cover, and steep for 10 minutes. Do not strain.

FOR THIS INFUSION, ERIN SUGGESTS MAKING

Ginger-Berry Soother

A zingy-sweet tea that's good for the tummy. SERVES 4 TO 6

🔹 1 recipe **Ginger and Raspberry Infusion**
(about 4 cups)

5 teaspoons loose-leaf (or 4 teabags)
green tea

2 to 4 tablespoons honey, to taste

Add the green tea to the Ginger and Raspberry Infusion, replace the cover, and continue to steep an additional 5 minutes.

Strain the Ginger-Berry Soother into individual cups or a teapot. Press gently on the raspberries to extract all the juice. Add the honey, stir until dissolved, and serve.

Alternatively, strain tea into a pitcher. Chill well and serve over ice.

Mango-Lemongrass Iced Tea

This tropical-fruit smoothie-style tea is so refreshing on a hot summer afternoon.

SERVES 4

1 medium-sized ripe mango

1 stalk lemongrass

1-inch piece fresh ginger

2 lime slices

7 teaspoons (or 6 teabags) loose-leaf fruity green tea

4 cups water, divided

2 tablespoons honey or agave nectar, or to taste

Cut the mango into chunks (see How to Cut Up a Mango). Place chunks in a medium bowl.

Peel away and discard any dry outer leaves of the lemongrass. Cut off the bottom 2 to 3 inches and discard. Crush and bruise the remaining lemongrass stalk by laying the side of a wide knife across the stalk and smashing it with the palm of your hand. Add the lemongrass to the mango chunks.

Peel and roughly chop the ginger. Add it to the bowl along with the lime slices.

Place the tea in a teapot or heat-resistant measuring cup. Bring 2 cups of water to just under a boil in a teakettle or saucepan. Pour the hot water over the tea. Steep for 2 to 3 minutes, agitating the infuser or teabags regularly.

Remove the infuser or teabags, and pour the still hot green tea over the fruit and steep for 15 to 30 minutes.

Remove the lemongrass and lime slices and discard. Purée the mango and tea mixture in a blender until smooth. Add the 2 remaining cups of cool water and honey and purée to blend. Taste and add additional honey, if desired.

Pour the blended fruit tea into a pitcher and serve over ice.

How to Cut Up a Mango

Mangos can be tricky to cut. They have a large pit in the center, and the flesh is slippery. If you look at a mango you will notice that it has a broad disk shape; the oval pit follows the shape of the mango. Place the unpeeled mango on your cutting board along one of its narrow edges. Slice the mango, on either side of the flat pit to remove the two "cheeks," then use a paring knife to cut crosshatch marks into the fruit. Bow the skin outward and cut away the chunks of fruit.

Peach-Infused Simple Syrup

Making a fruit-infused simple syrup is a great way to capture the sweetness of summer. You can use it for iced tea or try mixing it in sparkling water for a soda!

1 cup granulated or demerara sugar

1 cup water

1½ to 2 cups peeled and diced peaches, about 2 large

Bring sugar, water, and the diced peaches to a boil in a medium saucepan. Lower heat, cover, and simmer for 30 minutes, stirring occasionally and crushing the peaches with a spoon to extract as much flavor as possible.

Remove from heat, and let steep, covered, for an additional 30 minutes.

Strain the syrup through a fine-mesh strainer, and then use a funnel to pour it into a sterilized bottle, pressing the fruit against the strainer to extract more juice. The strained fruit can be used for shortcake, if you like.

Unused peach syrup can be refrigerated for up to 1 month.

FOR THIS INFUSION, ERIN SUGGESTS MAKING

Peach Iced Tea

SERVES 4 TO 8

8 cups water

⅓ cup loose-leaf (or 16 teabags) black tea

💧 **Peach-Infused Simple Syrup, to taste**

While the Peach-Infused Simple Syrup is steeping, brew your tea. Bring the water to just under a boil. Place the tea in a spouted bowl or saucepan. Pour the hot water over the tea, stir gently to blend, and steep for 4 to 5 minutes.

If you used loose-leaf tea, strain out the tea, or remove the teabags and pour the tea into a pitcher. Refrigerate until the tea has completely cooled.

When you are ready to serve, add the Peach-Infused Simple Syrup to the tea, a little at a time, until you like the sweetness. Or, serve the syrup separately so that everyone can add as much as they like. Serve the tea over ice.

Fruit Syrups for Tea & Cocktails

This recipe is for "basic" fruit-infused simple syrup. You can make "rich" simple syrup by doubling the amount of sugar. Rich syrup is sometimes preferable for cocktails. MAKES 1½ TO 2 CUPS

  1 cup granulated sugar

  1 cup water

  2 cups ripe fruit (see Erin's Tip)

Bring the sugar, water, and fruit to a boil in a medium saucepan. Lower the heat and gently crush the fruit to extract the juice. Continue to simmer, stirring, until the sugar has dissolved. Remove the pan from the heat, cover, and infuse for at least 30 minutes.

Strain the finished syrup through a fine sieve or mesh strainer. Press the fruit gently with a wooden spoon or spatula to express all the juices.

Store in a sterile bottle, covered, in the refrigerator for up to 1 month.

Erin's Tip: Try any fruit you like! You can choose one or mix and match. I find that berries, stone fruits, and tropical fruits impart the most flavor. My favorite berries are blueberries, strawberries, and blackberries, but don't limit yourself. For stone fruit, I love cherries, peaches, plums, and apricots at the height of ripeness. Tropical fruits make wonderful syrups too. I like using pineapple, mango, passion fruit, and guava.

Cold-Brewed Blueberry Iced Tea

This is my favorite iced tea! There's just something about the partial sweetness of the blueberries that complements the tannins of the black tea; it's like no other iced tea I've tried. I prefer the cold infusion because the fruit tastes fresher, but I've given you a quicker option if you are in a hurry. SERVES 8

2 cups fresh or frozen blueberries

½ cup freshly squeezed lemon juice

¾ cup caster sugar (see page 41)

8 cups water, divided

5 tablespoons (or 10 teabags) loose-leaf black tea

Lemon twist (rind strips) for garnish, optional

Place the blueberries, lemon juice, and caster sugar in a blender or food processor. Purée until smooth. Add 1 cup of water and purée until blended and the sugar is dissolved. You may need to scrape the sides of the blender to incorporate all the fruit pulp.

Strain the fruit juice through a fine-mesh strainer into a pitcher.

Add the remaining 7 cups of water and the tea. Cover and refrigerate until the tea has reached the flavor you like—usually 8 to 12 hours. Remove the teabags if you use them, or strain. Serve over ice garnished with lemon twists.

Option: The Quick Method

Place the blueberries and lemon juice in a medium saucepan. Cook slowly over medium heat until the blueberries are bursting and the mixture is simmering. Remove from the heat. Cover and let stand for 10 minutes.

Pour through a fine-mesh strainer into a small bowl, using the back of a spoon to squeeze out the juice. Discard the blueberry pulp. Rinse your saucepan clean.

Bring the water to just under a boil in the same saucepan. Add the tea and infuse for 5 minutes.

Strain out the tea or discard the teabags. Stir in the sugar and blueberry juice mixture. Pour into a pitcher; cover and chill 1 hour. Serve over ice. Garnish, if desired.

Chai with Fresh Herbs

Chai is simply the word for "tea" in many parts of the world. These days it's become synonymous with the sweet, spicy milk tea of India. SERVES 2 TO 3

1 cinnamon stick

¾ teaspoon whole black peppercorns

3 whole cloves

3 green cardamom pods

2 segments of star anise pod

½-inch piece fresh ginger, thinly sliced

3 tablespoons brown sugar, or to taste

2 cups water

3 teaspoons loose-leaf (or 2 teabags) strong black tea such as Assam

1 cup whole milk, coconut milk, or soy milk

4 to 6 fresh holy basil or mint leaves, torn

Combine cinnamon stick, peppercorns, cloves, cardamom, and star anise in a mortar and crush slightly. Don't make them into a powder. Alternatively, you can combine the spices in a sandwich bag and crush lightly with a mallet or the back of a spoon.

Pour the spices into a small saucepan. Add the ginger, brown sugar, and water. Bring to just under a boil over high heat. Reduce heat immediately to medium-low and simmer, partially covered, for 10 minutes.

Remove from heat. Add teabags and steep 5 minutes. Remove teabags.

Return the pan to the heat. Add milk and herbs, and heat tea just to simmer over high heat, whisking until sugar dissolves. Strain chai into mugs and serve hot.

Erin's Tip: Ceylon or "true" cinnamon has a milder, sweeter flavor than cassia cinnamon. Cassia cinnamon is more common in the United States and is spicier. Either can be used in this recipe, though I prefer Ceylon cinnamon in this tea because it doesn't overpower the other spices.

Reading the Leaves: A Brief Overview of Tea

Although we use the term "tea" to describe many steeped beverages, a true tea must be made from the tea plant, *Camellia sinensis*. Legend has it that tea was discovered in China almost five thousand years ago. Over the millennia, tea has gone from a medicinal treatment to status symbol to everyday beverage.

The most common varieties of tea are white, green, oolong, and black.

WHITE TEAS are the least processed and purest of the teas. Made from the tea buds and youngest leaves of *Camellia sinensis*, white tea is generally delicate in flavor and light in color, since the buds and leaves are simply steamed and dried. It's also the lowest in caffeine.

GREEN TEAS are the most popular teas in China and Japan, prized for their health benefits. The leaves are dried and then heat treated by roasting or steaming to stop fermentation. After the heat treatment, green teas are often rolled and dried again. Green teas range from yellowish green with toasty notes to deep green with grassy notes, depending on the heat treatment. Green teas are often combined with flowers or fruits to enhance their flavor.

OOLONG TEAS are probably most recognizable as the tea served in Chinese restaurants. During the harvest, the tea leaves are intentionally bruised or damaged by shaking. As the tea leaves dry and oxidize, the bruised edges turn reddish and the leaves become yellow. The oxidation process (also referred to as fermentation) is stopped by heat treatment, usually pan roasting. The more oxidized the leaves, the stronger the flavor of the tea. In general, oolong teas are full bodied with a sweet aroma.

BLACK TEAS are fully oxidized (fermented) and dried, which generally make them stronger and more full bodied than their less oxidized counterparts. In Western countries, black tea takes its name from the color of the tea leaves, while in China and many of its neighboring countries, black teas are often referred to as red teas for the color of the brew.

While green teas can lose their flavor within a year, black tea can be shelf stable for several years.

We've probably all heard of the health benefits of green tea. But according to tea associations in the United States, Canada, and Britain, black tea still accounts for 85 percent of all Western tea sales.

The Arnold Palmer (AKA the Half-and-Half)

When you are making iced tea, chill the tea completely before pouring over ice. That way you can use less tea, as I've done in this recipe. If you are in a hurry, double the amount of tea and pour over ice immediately after brewing.

SERVES 8 TO 10

1 cup granulated sugar

10 cups water, divided

Zest and juice from 5 to 6 large lemons (1 cup freshly squeezed lemon juice)

2 tablespoons loose-leaf (or 5 teabags) medium-bodied black tea, such as English breakfast

8 to 10 lemon slices for garnish

Combine sugar and 1 cup water in a medium saucepan. Cook over medium-high heat, stirring occasionally, until the sugar has dissolved and the mixture is simmering, about 5 minutes.

Remove the saucepan from the heat and stir in the lemon zest. Cover and steep for 10 minutes.

Stir in an additional 4 cups of water and the lemon juice. Strain through a fine strainer into a pitcher to remove the lemon zest. Refrigerate the lemonade until ready to serve.

Place the remaining 5 cups of water in a medium saucepan. (You can use the same one that you used for the lemonade syrup.) Heat the water over high heat until it is just under a boil. Remove the pan from the heat and add the tea. Steep the tea for 5 minutes. Strain out the tea leaves or remove the teabags. Pour the tea into a pitcher and refrigerate until chilled, about 1 hour.

Fill tall glasses with ice. Pour in chilled lemonade until the glass is half full. Fill the remainder of the glass with chilled tea. Garnish with a lemon slice and serve.

Alternatively, you can fill a pitcher with ice and lemon slices. Add the chilled tea and lemonade and stir to blend. Serve.

Erin's Tip: Warm lemons release more juice. You can pop them in the microwave, or blanch them in a pot of boiling water, for 30 seconds to 1 minute before juicing.

Extracts & Bitters

2

BOTANICAL INFUSIONS, including extracts and bitters, are one of the oldest forms of medicine. Simple tinctures (alcohol-based extracts of medicinal herbs) are still used as homeopathic treatments around the world today. Bitters (combinations of aromatic herbs and spices with bitter roots and barks) were used as treatments for everything from stomach upset to mood disorders.

Somewhere along the line we moved from focusing on health to focusing on flavor. So, though the vanilla extract in your cupboard may increase libido, chances are you are mainly using it for cookies (which I understand can also increase libido in some individuals!). When it comes to extracts, you can't beat the pure essence of natural flavors.

In addition to purity of flavor, extracts are one of the easiest infusions to create. All you need are patience and time. The results are phenomenal. One of the most stunning examples for me was homemade almond extract; in a side-by-side taste test, a high-quality commercial brand tasted shockingly chemical in comparison to the aromatic, bittersweet homemade version.

As for bitters, they are definitely back in vogue these days. At one time there were hundreds of bitters manufacturers in the United States, but Prohibition virtually wiped them off the map. For most of the 20th century, when we thought of bitters we thought of Angostura or, perhaps, Peychaud's Bitters. With the resurgence of a cocktail culture, we're seeing a flood of new bitters lines on the market. Bartenders and amateur mixologists alike confirm that although bitters are generally used in small amounts, the impact on a drink can be monumental.

Bitters are only slightly more complicated than extracts. You can create bitters by blending individual extracts, but that can be daunting for beginners. So I've created a series of bitters recipes from blends of aromatic spices, fruits, vegetables, and bittering agents. After you've tried your hand at the recipes in this chapter, I'm sure you'll be inspired to come up with your own creations. It's so much fun to experiment. If you start your own line, be sure to send me a sample or two!

Vanilla Extract

You can use alcohol other than vodka as your infusion base. I've tried rum and brandy, both of which impart a light caramel flavor to the vanilla. MAKES 1 CUP

5 to 7 vanilla beans

1 cup 80-proof vodka

To get the most flavor from your extract, split the vanilla beans lengthwise and place them in a small, sterile jar or bottle with a tight-fitting lid. It's important that the vanilla beans remain completely submerged in the vodka, so you may need to cut the vanilla beans into smaller sections.

Add the vodka. Close the lid securely and shake gently to blend. Place your jar in a cool, dark location for 8 weeks. Shake the jar every few days, always making sure the beans are fully submerged. You can use a spoon to push them under the vodka if they pop up.

At the end of the 8 weeks, remove the vanilla beans. Place them on a piece of paper towel and set aside to dry. You can use the beans for vanilla sugar (see Erin's Tip).

You'll notice some vanilla seeds in the liquid that have come loose from the pods. If you'd like, you can filter out the seeds by pouring the extract through a fine-mesh sieve lined with 3 or 4 layers of cheesecloth, but it certainly isn't necessary.

Your vanilla is ready to use and will keep for up to 1 year if stored properly. I suggest storing all extracts in an airtight dark bottle or, at the very least, in a dark cupboard. Storing under darkened conditions can help to keep the essential oils in the extract from dissipating in sunlight.

Erin's Tip: Once the vanilla beans have dried, you can use them to make vanilla sugar. (My husband loves vanilla sugar in his morning coffee.) After a couple of hours or so of drying, place the vanilla beans in a canister with 3 to 4 cups of sugar. Seal the canister and allow the vanilla beans to perfume the sugar for 1 to 2 weeks. For even more vanilla flavor, you can grind the dried vanilla beans in a food processor with ½ cup of sugar until they are pulverized. Then mix the ground vanilla beans and sugar with the remaining 2½ to 3½ cups of sugar, and seal in a canister to retain the freshness.

Vanilla Beans Terroir

You know the saying, "That's so vanilla"? It's kind of a slam, right? Like, that is *so* plain, everyday, boring. Well, whoever came up with that saying didn't know beans about vanilla! While researching this book I came across the coolest website called Beanilla (see Resources, page 172), which offers vanilla beans from around the world—each with unique flavor characteristics.

You may have heard of Madagascar Bourbon vanilla, which is noted for its dark, almost buttery sweetness, or Tahitian vanilla with chocolatey, caramel flavors, but how about vanilla beans from Uganda or Tonga or Mexico? Vanilla is as varied as wine; its character is influenced by its terroir (the characteristics of where it's grown).

I suggest experimenting—make some single varietals or try custom blends. Maybe you'd like a vanilla that's earthy with milk chocolate undertones. How about one that's fruity with dark-cherry or wine notes? Perhaps you'd prefer something a little smoky?

Think of how special a gift of homemade vanilla extract would be with a note about the type of vanilla beans you chose, and why. Include a recipe that highlights the flavor of your extract for the perfect extra touch.

Lemon Extract

This recipe calls for infusing lemons using vodka and caster sugar (superfine granulated sugar). If your local grocer doesn't carry caster sugar, you can make it yourself. Check the sidebar for details. MAKES ½ CUP

1 large lemon, organic if possible

1 teaspoon caster sugar

½ cup 80-proof vodka

Wash and dry the lemon. Using a channel knife (see page 120) or vegetable peeler, peel strips from the lemon. Try not to get too much of the white pith or your extract will become bitter.

Place the strips of lemon peel into a small, sterile Mason jar. Add caster sugar and vodka. Secure the jar lid and shake to dissolve the sugar.

Steep the extract in a dark place for 4 to 6 weeks, shaking occasionally. Remove the peel and it's ready to use!

You can store lemon extract in a dark bottle or cupboard, tightly closed, for up to 6 months.

Variation: Orange Extract

Substitute the peel from a medium orange for the lemon. I like to use Valencia oranges, but a navel orange would be fine too.

How to Make Caster Sugar

If you're an iced tea or coffee drinker, you'll love caster sugar, because it dissolves quickly, even in cold liquids. Sometimes called baker's sugar, it blends easily into batters and creamy desserts such as ice cream, crème brûlée, and more.

Making caster sugar is simple. All you do is place a cup or more of granulated sugar in a food processor. Cover the food processor with a clean kitchen towel. During the processing some of the sugar dust will aerate, so covering the food processor with a towel will help keep the kitchen clean.

Process on high for 1 minute, until the sugar is finely ground and slightly powdery. Let the sugar settle in the processor for a minute before removing the towel. Your caster sugar is ready to use.

Almond Extract

Traditionally, almond extract was made from bitter almonds. These days most commercial extracts are made from an infusion of almond oil that's a combination of bitter-almond oil and the oil from kernels of apricot pits and the pits of other stone fruit such as peaches or cherries. MAKES ⅔ CUP

¼ cup apricot kernels or raw bitter almonds, if available

⅔ cup 80-proof vodka

Place the apricot kernels in a glass, ½-pint Mason jar. Add the vodka. Close the lid and place in a pantry for 2 to 3 months. Shake the jar every couple of days.

When the strength of the almond extract is where you like it, pour the extract through a double-thickness cheesecloth-lined funnel into a clean bottle. If the extract is still cloudy, pour it through another layer of cheesecloth.

Erin's Tip: You can purchase apricot kernels online or crack apricot pits to extract them yourself. The easiest way to extract the kernel is to lay apricot pits on a hard, stable surface. Cover the pits with a kitchen towel and bash them with a hammer. When the pit splits open, you'll see what looks like an almond. That's the kernel. Or you can use a nutcracker. You'll need about 30 for ¼ cup.

Almond Cherry Fool with Almond Brittle

A fool is a simple dessert of cream and fruit. This one is particularly nice because you can serve it year-round using frozen cherries. SERVES 4

1¼ cups granulated sugar, divided

2 cups pitted dark sweet cherries, fresh or frozen

¼ cup brandy

💧 ½ to 1 teaspoon **Almond Extract**, divided, to taste

2 tablespoons water

1 cup blanched, sliced almonds

1 tablespoon butter, softened

1 cup heavy cream

Combine ½ cup sugar, cherries, and brandy in a high-sided saucepan over high heat. Bring to a boil, and cook until the mixture becomes thick and syrupy, about 15 to 20 minutes. Remove the cherries from the heat and stir in ¼ to ½ teaspoon Almond Extract. Stir until blended and transfer the cherries to a bowl. Refrigerate the cherries until chilled, about 1 hour.

To Make the Brittle: While the cherries are cooling, use the softened butter to grease a rimmed baking sheet and a rubber scraper. Set aside.

Blend the remaining ¾ cup sugar and water in a small, high-sided saucepan. Cook over medium-high heat until the sugar melts and begins to caramelize, about 10 to 15 minutes. *Do not stir during the heating time!*

When the sugar has caramelized, remove the pan from the heat. Quickly stir in almonds. Working quickly before the sugar has time to harden, pour the almond brittle into the buttered baking sheet. Spread the mixture with the buttered spatula as thinly and evenly as you can.

Set the almond brittle aside to cool completely, about 45 minutes. When the brittle is crisp and firm, break it into bite-size pieces.

Combine the cream and remaining ¼ to ½ teaspoon of Almond Extract, whip to firm peaks, and fold in half of the chilled cherries.

Divide the cherry whipped cream among 4 small dessert cups. Top with the remaining cherries and some broken brittle pieces. Serve immediately.

Erin's Tip: You can cook the cherries and make the brittle one day in advance. Store the cherries, covered, in the refrigerator until ready to use. Store the almond-brittle shards in an airtight container in a cool, dry location.

Mint Extract

It's simple to infuse mint to create mint extract, which can be used in ice creams, frostings, iced teas, and baking. MAKES ¾ CUP

¼ cup firmly packed fresh mint leaves, traditionally peppermint

¾ cup 80-proof vodka

Wash the mint leaves and pat dry or spin in a salad spinner. Gently crush the leaves in your hands.

Place the mint leaves in a sterilized, wide-mouth, ½-pint Mason jar. Add the vodka. Close the lid snug, and shake well to combine.

Place the jar in a cool, dark location. Shake several times a week to maximize the extraction. At first you may notice a few of the leaves floating at the surface, but over time they'll become fully saturated with alcohol and stay immersed. Allow the mint to infuse for 4 weeks.

Strain the mint leaves through a cheesecloth-lined strainer into a measuring cup. After you've poured the extract through the cloth, gather the edges and squeeze the leaves to extrude all the liquid. If you notice specks of mint in your extract, filter it again through more cheesecloth.

Pour your filtered extract into a small bottle with a snug-fitting lid. Store in dark bottle or in a dark cupboard for up to 6 months. Be sure to shake the bottle before each use.

Erin's Tip: If you'd like an even stronger mint extract, repeat the infusion process using the first batch of extract as the base. Simply strain the leaves as described. Then, repeat the infusion process by adding freshly crushed mint leaves to the extract. Steep in a sterilized, wide-mouth Mason jar for an additional 4 weeks. As before, shake the jar from time to time. Strain and store as directed above.

Rhubarb Bitters

The tartness of rhubarb makes it a natural to infuse for bitters. I like to add Rhubarb Bitters to a Cosmopolitan. Try a few dashes in your Ginger Ale too (page 81).

MAKES ABOUT 3 CUPS

2 cups diced fresh rhubarb stalks (about 2 stalks)

2 tablespoons chopped dried sweet orange peel

½ teaspoon whole cloves

4 whole allspice

½ teaspoon grains of paradise

½ teaspoon dried angelica root

½ teaspoon dried gentian root

2 cups 151-proof vodka or grain alcohol such as Everclear

1 cup filtered water

2 tablespoons honey

Place rhubarb, orange peel, cloves, allspice, grains of paradise, angelica root, and gentian root in a wide-mouth, quart-sized Mason jar. Add the vodka. Close the lid tightly and shake to blend.

Place the jar in a cool, dark location for 2 weeks. Shake the jar every couple of days. At the end of the 2 weeks, strain the contents through a cheesecloth- or muslin-lined funnel into another clean, wide-mouth jar. (Don't throw out the solids! You'll be using them again.) If you notice any residue in the strained liquid, repeat the process using fresh cheesecloth until the liquid is clear. Close the lid and store the alcohol-based infusion in a cool, dark cupboard.

Place the strained rhubarb and spices in a small saucepan. Add the water and bring to a boil. Remove from the heat. Cover the pan and allow it to steep until it reaches room temperature. Pour the cooled mixture into a sterilized wide-mouth jar. Close the lid and place the jar in a cool, dark cupboard for 1 week. Shake at least once a day.

Strain the rhubarb spice infusion through a cheesecloth-lined strainer or funnel into a liquid measuring cup. If you notice any sediment, strain the liquid through fresh cheesecloth until it's clear.

Add the strained rhubarb-spice infusion to the alcohol-based infusion. Add the honey and shake until well blended. Allow your bitters to rest for 3 to 5 days. Skim away any debris that floats to the surface. Funnel your bitters into smaller dark bottles. Store, away from direct sunlight, for up to 1 year.

Celery Bitters

I created this celery-infused bitters with Bloody Marys in mind, so they are spiced, citrusy, and herbaceous. MAKES 3 CUPS

1 sprig fresh thyme

2 one-inch-long strips of lemon zest, cut with a vegetable peeler

1 bay leaf, fresh or dried

¼ teaspoon white peppercorns

¼ cup celery seed

1 cup celery including leaves, coarsely chopped

½ teaspoon dried gentian root

2 cups 151-proof vodka or grain alcohol such as Everclear

1 cup filtered water

Put the thyme, lemon zest, bay leaf, peppercorns, celery seed, chopped celery, and gentian root in a sterile quart-sized Mason jar. Pour the alcohol over the celery and spices. Close the jar snugly and shake to blend. Let the mixture infuse in a dark place for 4 to 6 weeks, shaking daily.

After 4 to 6 weeks, strain out the celery and spices using a fine-mesh strainer. Discard the solids and pour the alcohol base back into the original jar. Add the water and shake to combine. Let stand in a dark place for 3 to 4 days.

Line a fine-mesh strainer with several layers of cheesecloth and strain out the solids. The bitters should be clear and debris free. If you notice any debris in the liquid, filter it again.

Transfer the strained bitters to small, dark bottles for storage. Store, away from direct sunlight, for up to 1 year.

Erin's Tip: It's a good idea to dip your cheesecloth into a little vodka before pouring the bitters through it. That makes the cheesecloth less absorbent. Be sure to wring out the cloth completely before lining the strainer.

Good Bloody Morning

After a particularly hedonistic night in my early twenties, I discovered that a blend of vodka and gin combine for a soothing (and flavorful) Bloody Mary.

MAKES 1 DRINK

- **Celery salt for the rim of your glass**
- **1 ounce vodka**
- **1 ounce gin**
- **5 ounces tomato, V-8, or Clamato juice**
- **1 teaspoon freshly squeezed lemon juice**
- 🌢 **2 dashes Celery Bitters**
- **Dash Worcestershire sauce**
- **Dash hot pepper sauce, optional**
- **Lemon wedge**
- **Pickled asparagus spear or pickled green bean, for garnish**

Place a teaspoon or two of celery salt on a side plate. Rub the lemon wedge around the edge of a tall glass to moisten it, and reserve the lemon wedge. Turn the glass upside down and spin the moistened edge in the celery salt to season the rim.

Fill the glass halfway with ice. Add the vodka, gin, tomato juice, lemon juice, Celery Bitters, Worcestershire sauce, and hot pepper sauce, if using. Stir to blend using a long iced tea spoon or drink paddle. Cut a notch in the lemon wedge and rest it on the rim of the glass. Garnish with a pickled asparagus spear or pickled green bean. Sip and prepare to face the day!

> **Erin's Tip:** Don't be stingy with your bitters dashes. I use an eye dropper and add the bitters little by little until I like the flavor.

Saffron Bitters

The infusion of these exotic flowers and spices creates a delicate bitters that work in perfect harmony with floral gins and brandy. The clean, astringent quality of quassia chips doesn't overpower the saffron and chamomile. MAKES ABOUT 1½ CUPS

1 teaspoon crumbled saffron threads

2 tablespoons dried chamomile flowers

1 whole cardamom pod

½ teaspoon whole coriander

¼ teaspoon dried sweet orange peel

¼ teaspoon quassia chips

1 cup 151-proof vodka or grain alcohol such as Everclear

½ cup filtered water

1 tablespoon honey

Place the saffron and chamomile in a wide-mouth, pint Mason jar.

Place the cardamom pod, coriander, and orange peel in a small muslin spice bag or tea sachet. Crush the contents with a whack or two from a smooth meat mallet or heavy pan. Place the bag with the crushed spices into the jar.

Place the quassia chips in another muslin spice bag or sachet and add it to the jar.

Add the alcohol. Close the jar lid securely and shake to blend. Place the jar in a dark location for 10 days, shaking daily.

At the end of the 10 days, remove the bag containing the quassia. Close the lid again and return the jar to its resting place for 4 more days. Continue to shake the jar daily.

At the end of 2 weeks, remove the second spice bag. Close the jar and continue to steep for 2 to 4 weeks, shaking occasionally.

After a total of 4 to 6 weeks has passed, strain the bitters base through a fine tea strainer to remove the saffron and chamomile. Return the alcohol to the original jar.

Place the saffron and chamomile in a small saucepan. Add the water and honey. Bring to a simmer. Remove the pan from the heat and allow it to cool to room temperature. Pour the contents back into the original jar with the bitters base. Close the lid and steep in a dark location for 1 additional week.

At the end of that week, strain the bitters through a cheesecloth-lined funnel into small, dark bottles. Store, away from direct sunlight, for up to 1 year.

Saffron & Cider

The smooth brandy and the light, sweet cider are balanced by the floral nature of the saffron bitters. MAKES 1 DRINK

2 ounces brandy

2 ounces apple cider

1½ teaspoons freshly squeezed lemon juice

¼ teaspoon simple syrup (see page 162)

◊ 4 healthy dashes **Saffron Bitters**

Combine the brandy, cider, lemon juice, simple syrup, and Saffron Bitters in an ice-filled cocktail shaker. Shake vigorously. Strain the cocktail into a martini glass.

Cherry-Vanilla Bitters

Whiskey infused with tart cherries and vanilla? Wow! These bitters just beg for bourbon. MAKES 1½ CUPS

¼ cup dried tart cherries

2-inch section vanilla bean

1 star anise

2 whole cloves

1 teaspoon dried sweet orange peel

¼ teaspoon wild cherry bark

¼ teaspoon cinchona bark

1 cup high-proof rye whiskey such as WhistlePig Straight Rye

½ cup filtered water

1½ teaspoons light molasses or turbinado sugar

Place the dried cherries, vanilla bean, star anise, cloves, and orange peel in a wide-mouth, pint Mason jar. Place the wild cherry and cinchona barks in a small muslin bag or tea sachet and tie it closed. Put the bag in the jar as well. Pour in the rye whiskey. Close the lid of the jar and shake vigorously to blend.

Store the jar in a cool, dry location. Shake daily for 10 days. Remove the muslin bag with the cherry bark and cinchona. Close the jar again and continue to infuse for another 10 days.

After the bitters have infused for almost 3 weeks, strain the contents through a fine-mesh strainer into a clean wide-mouth pint Mason jar. Add the strained cherries and spices to a small saucepan along with the water and the molasses.

Bring the mixture to a simmer over medium heat. When it has just begun to simmer, remove the pan from the heat, cover it, and allow it to cool to room temperature.

Pour the steep mixture into the jar containing the infused rye. Close the jar securely and shake to blend. Store the jar in a dark location for 2 weeks, shaking occasionally.

Strain the bitters through a cheesecloth-lined funnel into small, dark tincture bottles. They are now ready to use for your next Manhattan or favorite bourbon drink. Store, away from direct sunlight, for up to 1 year.

FOR THIS INFUSION, ERIN SUGGESTS MAKING

My Favorite Manhattan

MAKES 1 COCKTAIL

2 ounces bourbon

1 ounce sweet vermouth

2 dashes **Cherry-Vanilla Bitters**

1 Bada Bing Cherry (see Resources, page 172)

Measure the bourbon, sweet vermouth, and Cherry-Vanilla Bitters into a cocktail shaker. Add ice. Shake to blend. Allow the cocktail to rest a moment. Strain the Manhattan into a martini glass. Add a Bada Bing Cherry and serve.

Erin's Tip: Tim Metzger, owner of Tillen Farms, suggests his own infusion. Pour out half the juice from a jar of Bada Bing Cherries (reserve the juice for a Kir royale or an ice cream topping) and refill the jar with bourbon. Close the lid tightly. Turn the jar upside down, and refrigerate overnight. According to Tim, "You'll have arguably the world's finest bourbon-soaked cherry for a Manhattan or Old Fashioned." I'm inclined to agree.

Cranberry Bitters

Cranberry-infused whiskey makes a fantastic bitters. Try these bitters in a vodka-cranberry highball or a Negroni cocktail. MAKES 3 CUPS

1½ cups dried unsweetened cranberries

¼ cup sweet or bitter dried orange peel

1 tablespoon dried currants or raisins

½ teaspoon whole allspice

½ teaspoon whole cloves

1 whole star anise

2 cups high-proof rye whiskey such as WhistlePig Straight Rye

½ teaspoon cinchona bark

¼ teaspoon quassia chips

1 cup filtered water

2 tablespoons maple syrup

Place the dried cranberries, orange peel, and currants into a wide-mouth, quart Mason jar. Add the allspice, cloves, and star anise, then add the rye whiskey. Close the jar lid securely and shake to blend. Place the jar in a dark location for 14 days, shaking daily.

At the end of the 14 days, place the cinchona bark and quassia into a small muslin spice bag or tea sachet. Place the bag into the steeping spirits jar. Close the lid again and return the jar to its resting place for 14 more days. Continue to shake the jar daily.

After a total of 4 weeks have passed, remove the bag containing the cinchona bark and quassia. Strain the bitters base through a fine tea strainer to remove fruit and peel. Return the alcohol to the original jar. Close the lid and set aside.

Place the cranberries, orange peel, currants, and spices in a small saucepan. Add the water and maple syrup. Bring to a simmer. Remove the pan from the heat, cover, and allow it to cool to room temperature.

Pour the cooled fruit mixture into a sterile, wide-mouth, pint Mason jar. Close the lid and steep for 1 additional week.

At the end of that week, strain the fruit and spice mixture through several layers of cheesecloth into the alcohol base. Shake the mixture to blend. Let the jar rest for several days; if you notice any spice debris settling to the bottom of the jar, strain the bitters again.

Funnel into small, dark tincture bottles. Store, away from direct sunlight, for up to 1 year.

Cacao Bitters
with Cinnamon & Spice

This is one of my favorite bitters. The flavors mirror that of Oaxacan-style *mole negro*. These bitters add depth to chocolate dessert martinis and complement the flavor of spiced rum as well. MAKES 1½ CUPS

1 cup 151-proof vodka or grain alcohol such as Everclear

2 tablespoons cacao nibs

1 tablespoon raisins or chopped prunes

1 three- to four-inch-piece cinnamon stick

3 whole black peppercorns

1 whole clove

½ teaspoon whole anise seeds

½ teaspoon whole coriander seeds

½ teaspoon cinchona bark

1 ancho chili, stemmed, seeded, and torn into large pieces

½ cup filtered water

2½ teaspoons brown sugar

½ teaspoon maple syrup

Pour the vodka into a sterile, wide-mouth, pint Mason jar along with the cacao nibs and raisins. Close the jar and shake vigorously to blend. Store the jar at room temperature, away from direct sunlight, for 3 days. Try to shake the mixture at least once a day.

After 3 days, open the jar and add the cinnamon stick, peppercorns, clove, anise seeds, coriander, and cinchona bark. Close the jar again. Shake to blend. Steep for another 9 days, shaking the jar daily.

It's time to make one final addition to the bitters base. Add the ancho chili pieces to the jar. Close again, shake daily, and let steep for another 2 days.

Strain the bitters through a cheesecloth-lined, fine-mesh sieve or funnel into a clean, wide-mouth, pint-sized Mason jar. If you notice any debris in the strained bitters base, strain it again through fresh cheesecloth.

Combine the water, brown sugar, and maple syrup in a small saucepan. Warm gently over medium-low heat, stirring occasionally until the sugar has melted and is completely blended.

Add the sugar water to the strained bitters base. Close the jar and shake to blend. Although the mixture is complete, it's a good idea to let it rest for a day before transferring it to tincture bottles. This will allow any additional debris to sink to the bottom of the jar.

Funnel into dark tincture bottles and store, away from direct sunlight, for up to 1 year.

Orange Whiskey-Barrel Bitters

I love orange bitters, so I thought it would be fun to incorporate the toasty, vanilla, and caramel notes of a whiskey for these bitters. Adding the whiskey-barrel chips to the infusion provides even deeper, sweet smokiness to the bourbon base. MAKES 3 CUPS

2 cups high-proof bourbon such as 101-proof Wild Turkey Bourbon

Zest of 2 large oranges, peeled with a vegetable peeler

2 tablespoons dried orange peel (bitter or sweet, your choice)

1 tablespoon dried lemon peel

4 chunks whiskey-barrel chips (I used Jack Daniel's chips)

1 three-inch-piece cinnamon stick

1 whole star anise

3 whole allspice

½ teaspoon cinchona bark

½ teaspoon wild cherry bark

1 cup filtered water

2 tablespoons brown sugar

Add the whiskey, orange zest, dried orange peel, dried lemon peel, whiskey-barrel chips, cinnamon stick, star anise, allspice, cinchona bark, and wild cherry bark to a large, wide-mouth Mason jar. Close the jar and store at room temperature, away from direct sunlight, for 2 weeks. Shake the jar daily.

At the end of the 2 weeks, strain the contents of the jar though a cheesecloth-lined, fine-mesh strainer into a clean, wide-mouth quart-sized Mason jar. Close the jar and set aside.

Place the solids in a saucepan, add the water and brown sugar, and bring to a simmer over medium-high heat. Remove the pan from the heat. Carefully pour the contents back into the original wide-mouth jar. Allow to cool to room temperature. Close the jar securely, and store at room temperature, away from direct sunlight, for 1 week.

At the end of the week, strain the spiced water through a cheesecloth-lined funnel into the jar of liquor. Shake gently to combine. Close the lid and let the contents rest for 3 or 4 days. If you see any debris floating to the surface after 3 days, skim it away. If the mixture looks cloudy, filter it through a cheesecloth-lined funnel into small, dark tincture bottles.

Store, away from direct sunlight, for up to 1 year.

Orange-Infused Simple Syrup

MAKES 1 CUP

2 navel or Seville oranges

1 cup water

1 cup sugar

Wash the oranges to remove any waxy residue and pesticides. Use a vegetable peeler to remove the peel of the oranges in strips. (Try to remove only the orange peel; the white pith beneath is really bitter and will affect the flavor of your syrup.) Set aside.

Combine the water and sugar in a medium saucepan over medium-high heat. Stir occasionally until sugar dissolves.

Add the peel to the saucepan. Reduce the heat to medium-low and simmer for 30 to 40 minutes, until the syrup has thickened slightly.

Remove the orange peels, allow the infused syrup to cool to room temperature, and enjoy.

You can store the syrup in a covered bottle or jar in the refrigerator for up to 2 months.

FOR THIS INFUSION, ERIN SUGGESTS MAKING

Old-Fashioned

I love the flavor of orange in this cocktail, so I usually make it with Orange-Infused Simple Syrup, but plain simple syrup will do. MAKES 1 COCKTAIL

🌢 2 teaspoons **Orange-Infused Simple Syrup**

🌢 2 dashes **Orange Whiskey-Barrel Bitters**

2 dashes Angostura bitters

1 orange slice

Crushed ice

2 ounces bourbon

1 Bada Bing Cherry (see Resources, page 172)

Add Orange-Infused Simple Syrup, Orange Whiskey-Barrel Bitters, Angostura bitters, and the orange slice to an old-fashioned or rocks glass. Muddle the orange to release its juice and orange oil.

Fill the glass with crushed ice. Pour bourbon over the ice, and stir to combine. Garnish with a cherry.

Caraway Bitters

Caraway is great for digestive problems. Try these bitters with soda for an upset stomach, or in a gin or aquavit cocktail. MAKES 2 CUPS

¼ cup whole caraway seeds

2 teaspoons fennel seeds

1 teaspoon juniper berries

½ teaspoon whole allspice

¼ teaspoon quassia chips

1 cup 151-proof vodka or grain alcohol such as Everclear

1 cup filtered water

1 teaspoon turbinado sugar or demerara sugar

Place the first five ingredients into a sterilized, pint Mason jar. Add the vodka. Close the lid tightly and shake to blend. Allow the bitters to infuse for 2 weeks, shaking daily.

Strain the infusion through a fine-mesh strainer into a sterile, pint Mason jar. Place the solids in a small saucepan with the water and sugar. Bring the liquid to a simmer over medium heat, stirring occasionally.

Remove the pan from the heat and allow the liquid to cool to room temperature. Pour the infused water through a fine-mesh strainer into the jar containing the liquid. Close the jar again and allow the bitters to rest for 3 to 5 days. During that time, you will notice that some sediment settles at the bottom of the jar.

After the bitters have settled, line a fine-mesh strainer or funnel with several layers of cheesecloth. Filter the liquid through the cheesecloth into a dark tincture bottle.

Store, away from direct sunlight, for up to 1 year.

Bitter Truth

Each bittering agent imparts its own unique flavor. From tannic dryness to woodsy musk, they have distinct personalities. If you decide to experiment with creating your own bitters, you'll need to have a sense of what characteristics each brings to the table.

I used five bitter roots and barks in my recipes, including gentian root, quassia wood, cinchona bark, angelica root, wild cherry bark. Depending on the flavor I was trying to achieve, I occasionally blended them to add complexity. Here are brief descriptions of the flavors so you can choose what might be the best bitter flavor for your own creation.

Gentian Root is known to herbalists as one of the most bitter plants. If you taste the root, initial sweetness quickly gives way to a pronounced and lingering bitter flavor. I thought it was perfect in the Celery Bitters (page 46).

Quassia Wood has a relatively clean, astringent/tannic bitterness. I used it to add straightforward bitterness to the aromatic ingredients in Saffron Bitters (page 48), Caraway Bitters (page 56), and Caribbean-Rum Bitters (page 57).

Cinchona Bark has an earthy, bittersweet flavor with a slightly nutty finish. I thought it worked well with caramel, toasty, round flavors in the Cherry-Vanilla Bitters (page 50), Orange Whiskey-Barrel Bitters (page 53), and Cacao Bitters with Cinnamon and Spice (page 52).

Angelica Root is aromatic with subtle, musky sweetness in addition to the bitterness. I combined it with gentian root for the Rhubarb Bitters (page 45) to add balance and depth.

Wild Cherry Bark has a subtle, fruity, woodsy bitterness. I used it in conjunction with cinchona bark when I wanted to play up fruit and wood flavors in the Cherry-Vanilla Bitters (page 50) and Orange Whiskey-Barrel Bitters (page 53).

Caribbean-Rum Bitters

Try a dash of these bitters in a planter's punch or a Dark and Stormy cocktail.

MAKES 3 CUPS

2 cups high-proof rum such as Gosling's Black Seal or Bacardi 151

½ cup raisins

¼ cup dried sweet orange peel

¼ teaspoon whole allspice

4 whole cloves

1 one-inch piece fresh ginger, cut in half lengthwise

½ teaspoon quassia chips

3 tablespoons dark brown sugar or light molasses

1 cup filtered water

Combine rum, raisins, dried orange peel, allspice, and cloves in a wide-mouth quart Mason jar. Close the lid securely and shake to blend. Infuse, away from direct sunlight, for 1 week. Shake the jar daily to encourage deeper infusion.

After 1 week, place the piece of ginger and the quassia chips in a tea sachet or small muslin spice bag, and add to the mixture. Close the lid. Shake the jar to blend and allow to infuse for another week. Shake the jar daily.

At the end of the 2 weeks, strain the liquid through a fine-mesh strainer lined with several layers of cheesecloth into a clean, wide-mouth, quart-sized Mason jar.

Place the solids in a small saucepan. Add the sugar and water. Bring the mixture to a boil over medium-high heat. Cover the pan and remove it from the heat. Allow the mixture to cool to room temperature. Return the cooled mixture to the original jar and steep for 1 week. Try to shake the jar each day.

At the end of the week, strain the solids through a fine-mesh strainer into the rum base. If the mixture looks cloudy, strain it through a cheesecloth-lined funnel. Then funnel the finished mixture into small, dark tincture bottles.

Bitters can be stored at room temperature, out of direct sunlight, for 1 year.

Shrubs, Switchels & Kombuchas

3

WHEN YOU HEAR THE WORD "SHRUB," the first thing to pop into your mind might be a leafy green bush—not a beverage! But shrubs are making a big comeback.

Shrubs, also called sipping vinegars, were quite popular in Colonial America. To put them in modern terms, they were the Gatorade of the Colonial era, the precursor to soft drinks. It was thought that these sweet/tart beverages did a better job at slaking thirst than pure water. If you think about it, it makes sense. Sourness causes us to salivate. When we salivate, our mouths feel moist and we have the sensation of hydration.

I was first introduced to shrubs a few summers ago and was quite intrigued. Shrubs are typically combinations of sugar, vinegar, and fruit—though sometimes vegetables are used. For variety and complexity, aromatic spices and fresh herbs can also be added. What you end up with is a sweet-and-sour infused syrup that can be mixed with water, either still or sparkling, or blended with alcohol. Just as there's been a resurgence of interest in bitters, shrubs are showing up on cocktail menus everywhere.

I've included a switchel recipe as well. A "switchel," also called haymaker's punch, is another pre–Industrial Age refresher. As its name implies, these were often served to field workers. The flavor of my switchel may remind you of lemonade. It's an infusion of cider vinegar, lemon, ginger, maple syrup, and honey. It takes less time to make than a shrub and is a good introduction to vinegar-based beverages.

The final series of recipes in this chapter are kombuchas, Japanese fermented tea. I thought it was appropriate to include them in this chapter because they are sweet and sour as well. Kombucha is made by fermenting lightly sweetened tea. They are filled with probiotics, so they are revitalizing and healthful.

I hope you'll enjoy experimenting with these pre–soft drink beverages. Their complex flavors are exciting and sophisticated. Your kids may not like them, but I bet you will!

Blackberry-Vanilla Shrub **Pg 65**

Cucumber & Thai-Basil Shrub

This shrub was inspired by a traditional Thai condiment called *nam chim taeng kwa*. The spicy, sweet licorice flavor of the Thai basil really makes this shrub unique. But if you can't find Thai basil, try substituting mint instead.

MAKES 1½ CUPS (ENOUGH FOR UP TO 12 SERVINGS)

½ cup snugly packed, torn Thai basil leaves

1 cup rice vinegar

1 cup sugar

1 medium cucumber, peeled, seeded and diced (about 1½ cups)

Pinch cayenne pepper, optional

Place the Thai basil in a nonreactive, medium bowl. Set aside.

Place vinegar and sugar in a saucepan, and cook over medium heat, stirring until the sugar has dissolved.

Remove the saucepan from the heat, and pour the hot vinegar over the basil leaves. Allow the mixture to cool to room temperature, approximately 1 hour.

Stir the cucumbers and cayenne into the basil-vinegar infusion. Cover the bowl with a clean kitchen towel and let steep overnight.

Strain the mixture through a fine-mesh strainer into a sterile, wide-mouth, pint Mason jar. Discard the basil and cucumber chunks. (Or pick out the basil leaves and chill the cucumber chunks separately in a small bowl. Use as a fresh relish with a nice piece of fish.)

Close the jar and refrigerate the shrub mix for 1 week.

To serve, add 2 tablespoons or more of the Cucumber-and-Thai-Basil Shrub syrup to 8 ounces of sparkling or still water. Add ice and serve with a cucumber slice for garnish, if you like.

Store the shrub, covered, in the refrigerator for up to 1 week.

Tomato-Balsamic Shrub

Late-summer tomatoes straight off the vine are ideal for this shrub.

MAKES 4 CUPS (ENOUGH FOR UP TO 16 SERVINGS)

1 pound ripe tomatoes; choose sweet heirloom tomatoes such as Brandywine or Golden Jubilee

1¼ teaspoons coarse sea salt

½ cup granulated sugar

¼ cup fresh basil leaves, about 20 or so

2 tablespoons good-quality white balsamic vinegar

6 tablespoons good-quality white wine vinegar

Core and coarsely chop the tomatoes, and place them in a nonreactive bowl. Sprinkle the tomatoes with the salt and sugar, and use your hands to blend and squeeze the tomatoes to release their juices. Cover the bowl with plastic wrap and refrigerate at least 8 hours or overnight.

At the same time, place the basil leaves in a separate small, nonreactive bowl. Crush the leaves with your hands or a wooden spoon. Pour the balsamic and wine vinegars over the leaves, making sure the leaves are completely submerged. Seal the bowl with plastic wrap and allow to infuse overnight at room temperature.

Strain the tomatoes through a fine-mesh strainer into a third nonreactive bowl (a bowl with a pouring spout is great for this), pushing gently with your hands or a wooden spoon to release as much juice as possible. Discard the tomato pulp.

Next, strain the basil-infused vinegar through the fine-mesh strainer into the tomato juices. Stir to combine.

To serve, add 4 tablespoons of the Tomato-Balsamic Shrub syrup to 8 ounces of still or sparkling water. Stir to blend, and add ice. It's also nice blended with vodka.

Store the shrub, covered, in the refrigerator for up to 1 week.

Erin's Tip: I like the delicate floral sweetness of the white balsamic with the tomatoes, but you can substitute regular balsamic vinegar as well. The flavor will be a touch more raisin-y sweet.

Pineapple Shrub

This shrub is particularly good with some dark rum and a wedge of lime. MAKES 1 ½ CUPS (ENOUGH FOR UP TO 12 SERVINGS)

1 cup coconut vinegar or good-quality apple cider vinegar

1 cup turbinado sugar or demerara sugar

2 cups fresh pineapple chunks (see Erin's Tip)

1 teaspoon freshly squeezed lime juice

Combine the vinegar and sugar in a small saucepan. Cook, stirring occasionally, over medium heat until the sugar has completely dissolved. This should take about 5 to 10 minutes.

Remove the saucepan from the heat. Allow the mixture to cool to room temperature.

When the vinegar is cool, place the fresh pineapple chunks in a wide-mouth, quart Mason jar. Pour the cooled vinegar mixture over the fruit. Place the lid on the jar, close tightly, and shake.

Place the jar in the refrigerator and allow to infuse for 2 days.

Pour the shrub into a food processor or blender. Add the lime juice and purée the mixture to a coarse pulp. Strain the pulp through a fine-mesh sieve into a sterile, wide-mouth pint Mason jar. Discard the pineapple solids.

To serve, add 2 tablespoons of Pineapple Shrub syrup, or more to taste, to 8 ounces of sparkling water or coconut water. Stir to blend, and add ice.

Alternatively, add 2 tablespoons (or more to taste) of the shrub syrup to a cocktail shaker. Pour in 2 ounces of rum. Add a dash of Caribbean-Rum Bitters (page 57). Shake to blend and pour the mixture, including the ice, into an old-fashioned or rocks glass. Top with a little sparkling water and garnish with a wedge of lime.

Store the shrub, covered, in the refrigerator for up to 1 week.

Erin's Tip: *Don't* use canned pineapple! It has a tinny taste, and the added sugar from the syrup makes the shrub unbalanced.

Sugar . . . Aw, Honey, Honey

I use a number of different sugars throughout this book. It's worth talking about the differences because all sugar is *not* created equal. The way they are made and what they taste like can really affect a recipe. I figured you should know that there was method to my madness. Here's a rundown of the different sugars you'll see used throughout this book.

White Sugar (Granulated Sugar)
White sugar is highly processed, meaning washed, clarified, decolorized, evaporated, boiled to crystallization, and dried. (That's a shorthand version of sugar refining.) It can be made from sugarcane or sugar beets. I always try to purchase cane sugar. White sugar offers clean, pure sweetness that is easily incorporated or dissolved and doesn't overpower other flavors. Caster sugar (also called baker's sugar or superfine sugar) is finely granulated white sugar.

Unrefined Cane Sugar (*Rapadura*)
This natural cane sugar is prized for its caramel flavor. This is because the sugar is never separated from the molasses. It is far less processed than most commercial sugars. It's dehydrated at low heat, which helps with the retention of vitamins and minerals. Unrefined cane sugar can be substituted for granulated white sugar in most recipes, but I particularly enjoy it in root beer and vanilla soda.

Turbinado Sugar (Sugar in the Raw)
Known for its large, chunky amber crystals, turbinado sugar gets its name from the way it's processed. After the sugarcane is pressed, the water is slowly evaporated over low heat. The resulting sugar is spun in a centrifuge or turbine to dry it. It's closer to brown sugar than it is to white sugar because it is moister. Again, it's thought to be a little more healthful because it's less processed and retains more nutrients. It has a soft molasses flavor.

Demerara Sugar
Demerara sugar is similar to turbinado sugar in appearance, with its large, pale-golden crystals. Originally named for an area in Guyana where it was processed, demerara sugar is made from the first pressing of the sugarcane. The juices are steam heated to evaporate the water, leaving behind a thick syrup. That syrup is allowed to dehydrate further, which results in large crunchy crystals. Demerara sugar has a creamy, lightly molasses flavor similar to turbinado sugar.

Brown Sugar (Light and Dark)
Brown sugar is just white sugar with molasses mixed back in. Light brown sugar has less molasses. Dark brown sugar has more molasses. The molasses adds depth, but its flavor can be too much for certain recipes.

Coconut Palm Sugar (Coconut Sugar)
Not to be confused with palm sugar, coconut sugar is made from the sap of the coconut palm tree by boiling and dehydrating the sap. Its sugar is reputed to have a lower glycemic index than white sugar. It's not lower in calories, however. I use it in recipes that include other tropical ingredients such as coconut milk and tropical fruit. It feels like a more appropriate pairing.

Molasses
Molasses can be made from either sugarcane or sugar beets. Basically, it's the syrup that is left behind when sugar is extracted (that's incredibly oversimplified but...). It's a viscous sweetener ranging from "mild" or "light" molasses to the bitter-flavored "blackstrap" variety. When I've included molasses in recipes, I suggest using light molasses.

Maple Syrup
This north-woods staple is literally the sap of the sugar maple, red maple, or black maple tree. It's simmered to remove excess water, producing concentrated syrup. When purchasing maple syrup for the recipes in this book, I suggest looking for grade A light amber or medium amber syrup. Their mild flavors are best suited for these recipes. The darker syrups have a stronger flavor and are better for baking than infusions.

Agave Nectar (Agave Syrup)
Made from the *pina*, the pineapple-looking base of the agave plant (the same plant used for tequila), agave nectar has gained a lot of popularity as a low-glycemic sweetener. The thinking on that has changed due to its fructose levels, but I still use agave when I want a neutral-tasting sweetener for Latin American–inspired recipes like aguas frescas.

Raw Honey and Commercial Honey
In a nutshell (or a honeycomb), raw honey is unpasteurized and unfiltered. It's pretty close to the way it existed in the hive. To jar honey it must be warmed, but most producers of raw honey will not heat the honey to more than 118°F. This ensures that all the good stuff—natural enzymes and yeasts—aren't destroyed. Most commercial honeys are heated to 185°F to prevent crystallization, and then filtered to remove pollen, bee's wax, and so forth. They stay liquid, but they lose their health benefits. The moral of the story: If you are going to buy raw honey for health, be careful not to overheat it.

Honeyed Blueberry Shrub

Shrubs work very well with ripe and overripe fruit; even a little bruising is okay. Just make sure there is no mold on the fruit.

MAKES 3½ CUPS (ENOUGH FOR UP TO 28 SERVINGS)

3 cups ripe blueberries

⅛ teaspoon freshly grated nutmeg

1¼ cups turbinado or demerara sugar

¼ cup honey

2 cups good-quality apple cider vinegar

Rinse the blueberries under cold running water. Remove any stems.

Place the blueberries in a sterile, wide-mouth, ½-gallon Mason jar. Add the nutmeg, sugar, and honey. Using a wooden spoon or cocktail muddler, crush the berries until they burst and the sugar and honey are well combined.

Seal the jar and place it in a dark, cool location. Allow the fruit to macerate for 24 to 48 hours. If the weather is especially hot, you may want to refrigerate your fruit to keep it from fermenting.

Next, add the vinegar. Close the jar again and shake well. Store your shrub in a cool place for 7 to 10 days. Shake occasionally to be sure the sugar dissolves and blends.

When you are ready, place a strainer, over a nonreactive bowl (ceramic or glass is best). Pour the shrub through the strainer and use a muddler or wooden spoon to extract the last of the juice from the berries.

Line a funnel with several layers of cheesecloth and pour the strained shrub through the funnel into a sterile bottle.

To serve, add 2 to 4 tablespoons of the Honeyed Blueberry Shrub to a glass. Add 8 ounces of still or sparkling water and stir gently to blend. Add ice and enjoy!

Store the shrub, covered, in the refrigerator for up to 1 week.

FOR THIS INFUSION, ERIN SUGGESTS MAKING

Blueberry Kamikaze

Place 2 ounces Honeyed Blueberry Shrub, ½ ounce (1 tablespoon) Cointreau or triple sec, and 2 ounces vodka in a cocktail shaker. Add a dash of orange bitters, fill with ice, and shake. Pour the cocktail, including the ice, into an old-fashioned or rocks glass, or strain your kamikaze into a martini glass. Garnish with a few fresh blueberries and an orange twist.

2 ounces **Honeyed Blueberry Shrub**

½ ounce (1 tablespoon) cointreau or triple sec

2 ounces vodka

dash of orange bitters

Measure the ingredients into a cocktail shaker. Fill with ice and shake to blend. Pour the cocktail, including the ice, into an old-fashioned or rocks glass, or strain your kamikaze into a martini glass. Garnish with a few fresh blueberries and an orange twist.

Blackberry-Vanilla Shrub

See photo Pg 59. The turbinado sugar and honey add soft caramel sweetness to this shrub. I like to blend it with lemon sparkling water. MAKES 2½ CUPS (ENOUGH FOR UP TO 20 SERVINGS)

2 cups fresh blackberries

½ cup turbinado or demerara sugar

½ cup honey

½ vanilla bean

1 cup good-quality red wine vinegar

Place the berries in a medium bowl. Add the sugar and honey.

Use a potato masher or cocktail muddler to crush the berries. They don't have to be a mushy pulp, but crushing them a bit will increase the blackberry infusion. Cover the bowl with a clean kitchen towel and let stand 24 to 48 hours.

Next, split the vanilla bean and scrape the seeds. Place the scraped pod and seeds into a wide-mouth, pint Mason jar. Add the vinegar. Close the jar again and shake well. Infuse for 24 to 48 hours.

Strain the berries through a fine-mesh sieve into a sterile, wide-mouth, quart Mason jar. Press the berries with the back of a spoon or your hand to extract as much juice as possible.

Remove the vanilla bean pods from the vinegar. You may strain out the vanilla bean seeds as well, if you like. Add the vinegar to the strained fruit syrup. Close the jar securely and refrigerate for 1 week. Shake occasionally to be sure the sugar and honey fully dissolve and blend.

To serve, pour 2 to 4 tablespoons of the Blackberry-Vanilla Shrub syrup over ice and add about 8 ounces of still or sparkling, or lemon sparkling water. Stir to blend, and enjoy.

This shrub syrup can be stored up to 1 week in the refrigerator.

Plum–Star Anise Shrub

I love the combination of plums and star anise. I just couldn't resist putting them together for this shrub recipe. If anise is not your cup of tea, however, use a cinnamon stick and a couple of whole allspice instead.

MAKES ABOUT 2 CUPS (ENOUGH FOR UP TO 16 SERVINGS)

2 pounds ripe plums, pitted and diced (Italian plums or red plums are my favorites)

1 cup granulated sugar

2 whole star anise

1 fresh bay leaf

1 cup good-quality red wine vinegar

Place the chopped plums in a nonreactive bowl. Sprinkle with sugar. Add the star anise and bay leaf, and stir to combine. Cover the bowl with plastic wrap and refrigerate for 3 days.

After 3 days, add the vinegar. Cover the bowl with fresh plastic wrap and return it to the refrigerator for 1 day more.

Strain the shrub syrup through a fine-mesh strainer into a clean, wide-mouth, pint Mason jar. Refrigerate the mixture for 1 week before you use it.

To serve, add 2 to 4 tablespoons of the Plum–Star Anise Shrub syrup to a glass. Add 8 ounces of still or sparkling water, and stir gently to blend. Add ice, and enjoy!

In addition to sparkling or still water, this shrub is wonderful in champagne or dry sparkling wine!

Store the shrub, covered, in the refrigerator for up to 1 week.

FOR THIS INFUSION, ERIN SUGGESTS MAKING

Plum Shrub Sparkler

MAKES 1 DRINK

1 sugar cube

1 to 2 tablespoons Plum–Star Anise Shrub

Champagne or dry sparkling wine

Thin plum wedge for garnish, optional

Place the sugar cube in a champagne flute. Pour the plum shrub syrup over the sugar. Top with champagne and garnish with a plum wedge. Cheers!

Pear Shrub

This is a lovely shrub for fall. Try it with a touch of rum or brandy, if you like.

MAKES 2 CUPS (ENOUGH FOR UP TO 16 SERVINGS)

½ cup unrefined cane sugar or demerara sugar

¼ cup honey

1 cup good-quality apple cider vinegar

2 whole cloves

4 medium ripe pears

Pinch nutmeg

In a small, nonreactive saucepan, combine the sugar, honey, cider vinegar, and cloves. Cook over medium heat, stirring occasionally, until the sugar has dissolved. Remove the pan from the heat and allow the vinegar syrup to cool to room temperature, about 1 hour.

When the vinegar syrup has cooled, wash, core, and dice the pears. Place the diced pears in a medium nonreactive bowl. Pour the cooled vinegar syrup over the fruit. Add nutmeg and stir to blend.

Cover the bowl with plastic wrap and refrigerate for 1 day.

Strain the pears through a fine-mesh sieve into a clean bowl. Discard the pears and cloves. Funnel the vinegar syrup into a sterile, quart-sized Mason jar. Close the lid securely and refrigerate the mixture for 5 to 7 days before serving.

To serve, add 2 to 4 tablespoons of the Pear Shrub syrup to a glass. Add 8 ounces of still or carbonated water and stir gently to blend. Add ice and enjoy!

Store the shrub, covered, in the refrigerator for up to 1 week.

Erin's Tip: I usually select Bartlett or red Bartlett pears for their juicy nature, though any ripe pear will be delicious. For more information, read Pear Profiles on page 124.

Switchel (Haymaker's Punch)

In Colonial times it was thought that the sweet-and-sour switchel was more refreshing than plain water after you'd spent a long, hot day working in the fields.

SERVES 6 TO 8

6 cups water

½ to ¾ cup maple syrup

¼ cup honey or light molasses

3 tablespoons freshly squeezed lemon juice

¼ cup good-quality apple cider vinegar

2 tablespoons peeled and grated fresh ginger

Lemon slices, for garnish

Combine water, maple syrup, honey, and lemon juice in a medium saucepan. Warm over medium heat, stirring occasionally, until syrup and honey are fully blended, about 5 to 10 minutes.

Remove the saucepan from the heat, and carefully pour the sweetened water into a pitcher. Place the pitcher in the refrigerator to chill for at least 1 hour.

Pour the cider vinegar into a small nonreactive bowl or liquid measuring cup.

Stir the ginger into the cider vinegar, cover with a clean kitchen towel, and infuse for 1 hour.

Add the ginger-infused cider vinegar to the pitcher of syrup-sweetened water and stir well to blend. Serve over ice, garnished with lemon slices.

Peach Shrub

On my first visit to Venice, Italy, a friend insisted that I have a Bellini (peach nectar and champagne) at the famed Harry's Bar. Admittedly, it was an overpriced tourist trap, but the Bellini was *delightful*. This shrub makes a sweet-and-sour Bellini base for a fraction of the cost of lunch at Harry's. MAKES ABOUT 3 CUPS (ENOUGH FOR UP TO 24 SERVINGS)

> **2 pounds fresh peaches, peeled and pitted**
>
> **¾ cup caster sugar (see page 41)**
>
> **1 cup good-quality sparkling wine or champagne vinegar**
>
> **¼ teaspoon orange flower water, optional**

Place the peaches in a food processor and purée until smooth. Pour the peach purée into a nonreactive bowl. Stir in the sugar and vinegar. Cover the bowl with plastic wrap and refrigerate for 2 days.

Strain the purée through a fine-mesh strainer, pressing gently on the solids to express all the juice. Discard the pulp.

Pour the shrub into a wide-mouth quart-sized Mason jar. Add the orange flower water, if using. Close the lid securely and shake to blend. Refrigerate for 1 week before using. You may notice that the liquid separates while it's resting. Simply shake it gently to blend.

To serve, add 2 to 4 tablespoons of the Peach Shrub syrup to a glass. Add 8 ounces of still or sparkling water and stir gently to blend. Add ice and enjoy!

Store the shrub, covered, in the refrigerator for up to 1 week.

For the **Peach Shrub Bellini**, measure 1 to 2 tablespoons of Peach Shrub syrup into a champagne glass and top with prosecco or other sparkling wine.

SCOBY Scraps

SCOBY is an acronym for Symbiotic Culture of Bacteria and Yeasts. It is basically a collection bacteria and yeast species used in the fermentation of tea for kombucha. A healthy SCOBY will have a cloudy, gelatinous look to it. You may also notice strings of brownish yeast particles. This is perfectly normal. It will smell lightly of vinegar. If, however, you ever notice any black or green mold on the surface of the SCOBY, or a rancid, funky smell, throw it out immediately. It's probably due to an imbalance in the water-sugar-tea-starter ratio. A bad SCOBY is really rare, though, so don't worry too much.

You may be wondering where to get a SCOBY. I got my SCOBY from my friend Sarah, but if you don't know someone who is already making kombucha, there are a number of options. Many entrepreneurs are selling SCOBYs on the Internet and Craigslist. There are sites that sell dehydrated SCOBY that can be reconstituted to make kombucha.

You can also use raw (unpasteurized), unflavored kombucha purchased from a health food store or grocery store to grow your first SCOBY. Follow the basic recipe, adding the raw, unflavored kombucha in place of the mother and starter liquid. This does take a little longer to start (up to 4 weeks) but works well.

SCOBYs can be used multiple times. You'll notice the mother growing thicker with the addition of babies (new layers). From time to time, peel away the thicker, older layers and discard or compost them.

Ideally, you'll continue to brew a new batch of kombucha as soon as your previous batch is finished, but if you need to take a break between batches, it's best to store your SCOBY submerged in kombucha inside a glass jar or ceramic container. The cold temperature puts your SCOBY into a mild dormant state. Try not to wait too long. I recommend no longer than a month between batches, or your SCOBY may starve.

Basic Kombucha

Kombucha is a fermented tea. It's chock-full of gut-healthy probiotics. You can use almost any real tea (*Camellia sinensis*) to make kombucha, but you should avoid teas that contain oils and added flavoring. MAKES TWELVE 8-OUNCE SERVINGS

12 cups water, divided (If you have off-tasting tap water, consider using filtered water)

7 teabags or 3 tablespoons loose-leaf tea

1 scant cup (7 ounces) granulated sugar

1½ cups starter kombucha from an earlier batch (see SCOBY Scraps) or store-bought, raw, unflavored kombucha

1 SCOBY (symbiotic culture of bacteria and yeasts; see SCOBY Scraps)

Heat 4 cups of water in a large saucepan over high heat. When the water begins to simmer, remove the saucepan from the heat and add the tea. Cover and steep for 10 minutes.

When the tea has finished steeping, remove the tea and add the sugar. Stir until the sugar has dissolved. Add the 8 remaining cups of water. The water should be at room temperature, below 85°F. If not, allow it to cool slightly.

Pour the cooled tea into a clean, large (gallon-size) Mason jar or food-safe crock. I use a glass beverage dispenser with a spigot so I can test the kombucha without disturbing the SCOBY.

Add the kombucha starter. Wash your hands thoroughly; be sure there is no soap residue left behind. Gently pick up the SCOBY and lower it into the jar.

Cover the jar with a clean kitchen towel secured with string or a large rubber band. This will keep fruit flies out.

Place the jar in a warm location, away from direct sunlight. (I usually place my jar on top of the refrigerator.) Ferment the kombucha, undisturbed, for 7 days. If your location is warm enough, the kombucha should be ready. In colder months it can take 3 weeks or more depending

on how warm your home is. Kombucha ferments quickest between 78°F and 85°F.

During this time, your SCOBY will reproduce. You should see a filmy pancake growing above the mother attached by an umbilical cord of culture—a baby is born! A SCOBY baby may not be cute but it's social—in fact, it's a whole colony unto itself!

To see if your kombucha is ready, taste. The flavor should be slightly sweet and tangy tart. If the flavor is right, wash your hands and remove the SCOBY mother and baby.

Once your kombucha has reached a balance of sweet and tangy that you like, it's time to bottle it. First ladle out 1½ cups of kombucha to use as a starter for your next batch. Now, rinse your hands well, reach into the jar, remove the mother and baby SCOBYs, and place them on a clean plate. If you don't plan to start a new batch of kombucha immediately, save the SCOBY and the starter liquid in the refrigerator (see SCOBY Scraps).

Pour the remaining kombucha into sterile bottles, leaving at least an inch of headroom between the liquid and the cap. I like to use swing-top bottles to store my kombucha. Think old-fashioned beer bottle that has a metal clasp and stopper attached (like Grolsch Beer).

Some people like to strain out the cultures and cloudy bits of yeast during bottling. Whether you do is completely up to you. I figure the point of the drink is the probiotic culture, so I bottle it straight from the fermentation jar.

At this point your kombucha is ready to drink, but you can also do a secondary fermentation to add fizz (carbonation). If you don't want to carbonate, the secondary fermentation is optional. Simply bottle it as described and refrigerate it immediately. The cold significantly slows the fermentation process. Store for up to 1 month.

To add a little fizz through secondary fermentation, cap the bottle and allow it to sit at room temperature for a few more days (2 to 5 depending on how warm it is). This will cause a buildup of gases as the yeasts continue to multiply. After a day or two, open the cap. If you get a *pffft* sound of carbonation escaping, it's done. (Do be careful when opening the bottles. Remember the buildup of carbon dioxide is creating pressure; if you let it overferment, there is a chance the bottle could break. On that note, always inspect your bottles for cracks or imperfections before filling them.) Transfer the bottled kombucha to the refrigerator and store for up to 1 month.

The secondary fermentation is also when you experiment with additional flavors, as you'll see in the recipes for Ginger-Infused Green Tea Kombucha and Lavender-Infused Black Tea Kombucha.

Ginger-Infused Green Tea Kombucha

Adding ginger to the natural probiotics in kombucha can be an upset-tummy tamer.

MAKES TWELVE 8-OUNCE SERVINGS

💧 1 batch green tea **Basic Kombucha** (page 75)

3 tablespoons peeled and minced fresh ginger

If you haven't done so already, remove the SCOBY and about 1½ cups of kombucha to use to start your next batch. Set aside. Always remember to wash and rinse your hands well before handling the SCOBY.

Stir the ginger into the remaining kombucha. Cover the container with a clean kitchen towel. Secure the towel with some string or a large rubber band. This will keep fruit flies out of the tea. Allow to infuse for 2 to 4 hours.

At this point you have two options: you can strain (or not strain) the kombucha and drink some immediately while storing the remaining kombucha in bottles or jars in the refrigerator, or you can add fizz with a secondary fermentation. I love a little fizz in my kombucha, so I also do a secondary fermentation whether I'm infusing additional flavors or not.

If you choose to do a secondary fermentation, funnel the infused kombucha into sterile bottles. I prefer to use swing-cap bottles as described in the Basic Kombucha recipe. These bottles seal better than jars and lock in the carbon dioxide created by the fermenting yeast. A tighter seal equals more fizz.

Fill the bottles, leaving at least 1 inch of headroom between the kombucha and the cap. Allow it to sit at room temperature, out of direct sunlight, for a few more days (typically 2 to 5 depending on how warm it is). Kombucha ferments most quickly between 70°F and 85°F.

To test if the kombucha is carbonated enough, open the cap. If you get a *pffft* sound of carbonation escaping, chances are it's done. (Once again, be careful when opening the bottles.) Taste a little and if you like the effervescence, transfer the bottled kombucha to the refrigerator to chill.

You can store your kombucha in the refrigerator for up to 1 month.

Lavender-Infused Black Tea Kombucha

Lavender can be quite a strong flavor, so it's good to pair it with equally strong black tea for balance. MAKES TWELVE 8-OUNCE SERVINGS

 1 batch black tea Basic Kombucha (page 75)

3 teaspoons dried culinary lavender flowers

9 to 12 raisins, optional

If you haven't done so already, remove the SCOBY and 1½ cups kombucha to use to start your next batch. Set aside. Always remember to wash and rinse your hands well before handling the SCOBY.

Stir dried lavender into the remaining kombucha. Cover the container with a clean kitchen towel. Secure the towel with some string or a large rubber band. This will keep fruit flies out of the kombucha. Allow to infuse for 24 to 48 hours.

At this point you have two options: you can strain the kombucha, drink it immediately, and store the remaining kombucha in bottles or jars in the refrigerator, or you can add fizz with a secondary fermentation.

If you decide to do a secondary fermentation, funnel the infused kombucha into sterile bottles. Fill the bottles, leaving at least 1 inch of headroom between the kombucha and the top of the bottle. Add 3 raisins to each bottle depending on the size. I usually do my secondary fermentation in a larger bottle that holds about 3 cups of kombucha, so my ratio is 1 raisin per 8 ounces of liquid. The raisins provide a little sugar boost to get the fermentation going again, but they don't affect the flavor.

Seal the bottles and allow them to sit at room temperature, out of direct sunlight, for a few more days (typically 2 to 5 depending on how warm it is). Kombucha ferments most quickly between 70°F and 80°F.

To test if the kombucha is carbonated enough, open the cap. If you get a *pffft* sound of carbonation escaping, chances are it's done. (Always be careful when opening the bottles.) Taste a little and if you like the effervescence, transfer the bottled kombucha to the refrigerator to chill.

You can store your kombucha in the refrigerator for up to 1 month.

Erin's Tip: I like to use glass swing-top bottles to store my kombucha. A swing-top bottle is an old-fashioned beer bottle that has a metal clasp and stopper attached (think Grolsch Beer). I like them because they are durable, reusable, easy to close, and seal tightly. You have a few options for sourcing this type of bottle, including collecting used beer bottles from craft-brew-drinking friends or buying them at a brewing-supply store or online. During the holiday season, Trader Joe's carries nonalcoholic Triple Ginger Brew in a swing-top bottle. Each Ginger Brew bottle holds 750 milliliters (25.6 oz.). One batch of Basic Kombucha divides evenly among 4 bottles with about 2 inches of headroom in each. Regardless of the type or size bottle you choose, be sure to sterilize them before each use (see How to Sterilize Bottles, Jars, and Containers on page 15).

Soft Drinks & Infused Waters

4

OKAY, I'LL ADMIT IT. I spent years drinking diet soda. It started when I was in my 20s and so concerned about my weight. The idea of sugary soft drinks was really scary to me. Diet soda also allowed me to justify eating just about anything. I mean, just think of the calories I was saving!

Eventually, though, I began to think about the health ramifications of drinking all those chemicals. I didn't drink diet soda every day, but I drank it enough to wonder what the prolonged exposure might be doing to my body. And, despite that portrait stored in my closet (à la *Dorian Gray*), I am getting older. Like many people, I realize I can't keep eating and drinking the way I did when I was a kid, so I started to make adjustments. Making homemade sodas was one of them.

I'm not going to kid you; the core of most soft drinks is sugar, but there are two bonuses to consider. First, you can choose the *type* of sugar or other sweetener that you use. Some are considered more healthful than others. I give suggestions based on flavor profiles, but, ultimately, it's up to you. Second, with the exceptions of the Ginger Beer and Old-Fashioned Root Beer, you'll be making soft drink syrups. The cool part about that is you ultimately control how sweet your final soft drink will be. You can add as little or as much of the syrup as you like.

I've included a couple of unusual infusions for Hot Spiced Lemonade and Dandelion Punch. Hot Spiced Lemonade is infused by percolation. From the Latin word *percolare,* meaning "to strain through," percolation is mainly associated with coffee. I thought Hot Spiced Lemonade would be a fun way to explore a different form of infusion. The Dandelion Punch is a variation on a Quaker recipe from the 1800s that I found in a cookbook belonging to my great-grandmother. With the renewed emphasis on foraging, it seemed quite timely. Plus, it provides additional motivation to pull up those pesky dandelions that are threatening to take over your yard!

The last section of this chapter focuses on aguas frescas, fruit-infused water. Common throughout Mexico, the Caribbean, and Central America, agua fresca—literally translated as "fresh water"—is typically a lightly sweetened purée of water and fresh fruit. In most of the recipes, I've included a traditional agua fresca recipe as well as a simple infusion version. Both styles are tasty and thirst quenching, so you can't go wrong!

Strawberry-Basil-Infused
Simple Syrup **Pg 87**

Ginger Ale

I modeled this recipe after Q Drinks' ginger ale. It's sophisticated, intensely gingery, and spicy. Vince, my husband, can't get enough of it!

MAKES ABOUT 3 CUPS (UP TO TWENTY-FOUR 8-OUNCE SODAS)

2 ounces peeled and minced fresh ginger (a scant ½ cup)

2 cups boiling water

2 cups granulated sugar

1 tablespoon ground ginger

Pinch sea salt

1 tablespoon citric acid

Pinch cayenne pepper, optional

Carbonated water such as club soda, seltzer, or sparkling water

Place the ginger in a nonreactive bowl. Pour the boiling water over the ginger and set aside to infuse for 4 hours.

Strain the ginger infusion through a strainer into a nonreactive saucepan. Whisk in the sugar, ground ginger, and salt. Cook over medium-high heat until the sugar dissolves and the mixture begins to simmer.

Remove the pan from the heat. Stir in the citric acid and cayenne pepper, if using. Funnel the syrup into a sterile jar. Close the lid and refrigerate until the syrup is completely chilled, about 1½ hours.

Shake to blend before using. For a single drink, combine 2 tablespoons of ginger syrup, or more to taste, with 7 or 8 ounces of carbonated water.

Serve your ginger ale in a tall glass with lots of ice and a twist of lime or lemon peel, if you like.

The syrup can be refrigerated for up to 3 weeks.

Pucker Up! Citric Acid in Soda

If you read the labels of most soft drinks, you'll see citric acid listed as an ingredient. It adds just the right amount of tartness to balance out sweetness. As I experimented with various artisan soft drink syrups, in several cases I found I wasn't getting a needed acidity and balance from lemon juice and zest. Often, in an attempt to bring up the tartness, I'd cause the lemon flavor to dominate. So, I turned to citric acid.

Citric acid is an organic acid found in citrus (no surprise there). It not only provides sourness but also acts as a preservative and has been used in food production for more than 100 years.

You can typically find citric acid among the canning supplies in your local grocery store. If you don't find it, it's available online at suppliers such as Mountain Rose Herbs or Tenzing Momo (also see Resources, page 172).

Ginger Beer

The main difference between ginger ale and ginger beer is fermentation. With ginger ale, like most sodas, you add carbonated water to flavored syrup. The word "beer" implies fermentation, which is the case for both ginger beer and root beer. The CO_2 given off by the yeast creates carbonation.

MAKES SIXTEEN 8-OUNCE SERVINGS

7½ to 8 cups room-temperature filtered water, divided

1 cup caster sugar (see page 41)

2 tablespoons freshly squeezed lemon juice

2 tablespoons freshly squeezed lime juice

⅓ cup peeled and finely minced fresh ginger

¼ teaspoon dry active brewer's or champagne yeast

Add 1½ cups of room-temperature water to a larger liquid measuring cup. Add the sugar, lemon juice, and lime juice, and stir gently until the sugar has dissolved. Add the minced ginger and stir to blend.

Place a funnel in the neck of a clean, plastic, 2-liter bottle. (By the way, when carbonating sodas, I highly recommend using plastic bottles instead of glass. Plastic bottles are less likely to explode if they over-carbonate.) Add the yeast through the funnel into the bottle.

Pour the sugared ginger water through the funnel into the bottle. If the ginger clogs the funnel neck, coax it through with a toothpick or bamboo skewer. Cap the bottle and shake gently to combine and activate the yeast.

Open the bottle and place the funnel in the neck again. Measure and pour the remaining 6 or so cups of water from the same liquid measuring you used to mix the sugared water. This is so that any sugar residue left behind will be added to the soda. Leave about 1 inch of headroom between the ginger beer and the cap.

Cap the bottle tightly and let it sit in a warm location for 1 to 2 days. Invert the bottle once or twice a day to incorporate the ginger.

For fermentation, ideally the temperature should be above 75°F to active the yeast, so if it's a little cooler it may take more time to carbonate. After 24 hours, check to see if carbonation is building in the bottle by squeezing it slightly. If the bottle seems taut and resistant to pressure, the ginger beer is ready. Open the cap to see if it is carbonated enough for you. If not, let it sit a little longer.

Once the carbonation has reached the level that you desire, place the ginger beer in the refrigerator to chill for several hours. When you are ready to serve it, you can strain it through a fine-mesh strainer to remove the ginger if you like, but many ginger beers are unfiltered. Store in the refrigerator for up to 2 weeks.

Erin's Tip: It's awfully hard to control carbonation buildup in soft drinks. I recommend that you "burp" your ginger beer the first time you open it. Burping means that you loosen the cap slightly to release some pressure. You'll hear a little hiss if you've built carbonation. Tighten the cap after the hiss and allow the bubbles to dissipate a little. You may need to burp the bottle several times before you pour your first glass. I had a funny experience with my first batch of ginger beer: I opened the bottle too quickly and a geyser of ginger beer began to erupt. My panicked reaction was to put my mouth over the bottle and run to the kitchen sink. Needless to say, my husband got quite a laugh from my shenanigans. So, trust me on this.

Old-Fashioned Root Beer

This recipe is for root beer purists. A throwback unlike its modern counterpart, it has woodsy spice with a molasses-like finish. This is not your kids' root beer!

MAKES EIGHT 16-OUNCE SODAS

4 quarts filtered water, divided

1 tablespoon (¼ ounce) sassafras root

1 tablespoon burdock root

1½ teaspoons licorice root

½ to 1 teaspoon cinnamon chunks (I use 2 large Korintje Cinnamon Bark chunks from online retailer Spice Jungle; see Resources)

4 whole cloves

Pinch nutmeg

2-inch section vanilla bean

1½ cups turbinado sugar, unrefined cane sugar, or brown sugar

⅛ teaspoon champagne or ale yeast

Measure 2 quarts of water into a stockpot. Add the sassafras, burdock, licorice, cinnamon, cloves, and nutmeg. Bring the mixture to a boil. Reduce heat and simmer for 30 minutes. Remove the pot from the heat and add the vanilla bean. Cover the pot and steep for 30 minutes.

Strain the mixture through a cheesecloth-lined, fine-mesh sieve into a clean stockpot or 1-gallon crock. Add the sugar, and stir until dissolved.

Add 2 quarts of cool filtered water. Check the temperature. When the liquid has cooled to about 75°F, and no warmer than 84°F, stir in the yeast. Ferment for 1 hour.

Stir the root beer once again and funnel into 8 sterile, 16-ounce bottles or two 2-liter bottles. (Again, when carbonating sodas, I highly recommend using plastic bottles instead of glass. Plastic bottles are less likely to explode if they over-carbonate.) Store at room temperature for 1 to 5 days (depending on how warm your room is). Squeeze the bottles each day to gauge the buildup of carbonation. When the bottles feel noticeably taut, transfer them to the refrigerator. Refrigerate overnight to chill thoroughly before opening.

Erin's Tip: You can find sassafras, licorice, and burdock online at Tenzing Momo or Mountain Rose Herbs. See details in the Resources section on page 172.

Vanilla-Infused Soda Syrup

MAKES 1½ CUPS (UP TO TWENTY-FOUR 8-OUNCE SODAS)

- **1 vanilla bean**
- **1¼ cup turbinado sugar or granulated sugar**
- **1 cup water**
- **2½ teaspoons Vanilla Extract (page 40)**

Split the vanilla bean lengthwise and scrape the seeds from the pod. Cut the scraped pod into 2- to 3-inch sections.

Place the vanilla seeds and pieces of vanilla pod into a small saucepan. Add the sugar and water. Bring to a boil over medium-high heat, stirring constantly.

When the sugar is dissolved, remove the pan from the heat. Stir in the Vanilla Extract. Cover the pan and allow it to steep until it reaches room temperature, approximately 1 hour.

When the syrup is cool, remove the vanilla bean segments and discard. If you'd like, you can strain the syrup through a cheesecloth-lined funnel into a sterilized bottle to remove the vanilla flecks. (Personally, I like to leave them in the syrup.)

FOR THIS INFUSION,
ERIN SUGGESTS MAKING

Vanilla Soda

- 💧 **1 to 2 tablespoons Vanilla-Infused Soda Syrup, or to taste**
- **8 ounces carbonated water such as club soda, seltzer, or sparkling water**

Pour the Vanilla-Infused Soda Syrup into a tall glass and top with carbonated water. Stir gently with a long spoon to blend. Add ice and enjoy! Better yet, add 2 to 3 teaspoons of vanilla syrup to a highball glass, add a shot of rum, and stir to blend. Fill the glass with ice and top with carbonated water.

Lavender-Infused Soda Syrup

MAKES ABOUT 1½ CUPS (UP TO 12 8-OUNCE SODAS)

- **¾ cup honey or granulated sugar**
- **1 cup lukewarm water**
- **2 tablespoons dried culinary lavender flowers**
- **1 teaspoon finely grated lemon zest**

Pour the honey into a small saucepan. Scrape any honey sticking to the sides of the measuring cup with a rubber scraper. Then fill the same measuring cup with 1 cup of water. Stir the water gently with the rubber scraper and then pour it into the saucepan. Add the lavender and lemon zest.

Bring to a simmer over medium heat, stirring occasionally. Remove the saucepan from the heat. Cover and let steep for 10 minutes.

Strain the lavender syrup through a fine-mesh strainer into a sterile bottle. Store in the refrigerator for up to 5 days.

FOR THIS INFUSION,
ERIN SUGGESTS MAKING

Lavender Soda

- 💧 **2 tablespoons Lavender-Infused Soda Syrup, or to taste**
- **8 ounces carbonated water such as club soda, seltzer, or sparkling water**

When ready to serve, measure the Lavender-Infused Soda Syrup into a tall glass. Add carbonated water and stir gently to blend. Add ice and serve.

Strawberry-Basil-Infused Soda Syrup

See photo Pg 79. Basil pairs so naturally with strawberries!

MAKES ABOUT 1¼ CUPS SYRUP (UP TO SEVEN 8-OUNCE SODAS)

¾ pound fresh or frozen (thawed) strawberries, hulled

Water, as needed

2 tablespoons freshly squeezed lemon juice

¾ cup granulated sugar

⅓ cup loosely packed basil leaves

Purée the strawberries in a blender or food processor until smooth. Strain the purée through a fine-mesh sieve, pressing firmly on the pulp with a spoon or spatula. Discard the solids.

Pour the strained strawberry juice into a liquid measuring cup. Add water to reach 1 cup, if needed.

Pour the liquid into a small saucepan. Stir in the lemon juice and sugar. Cook over medium-high heat until the sugar has fully dissolved and the syrup is simmering. Remove the saucepan from the heat and stir in the basil leaves. Allow the strawberry-basil syrup to steep and cool, until it has reached room temperature.

Strain the syrup through a fine-mesh sieve into a sterilized bottle or jar (see note on page 15) and discard the steamed basil leaves.

Unused syrup can be stored in the refrigerator for up to 1 week.

FOR THIS INFUSION,
ERIN SUGGESTS MAKING

Strawberry-Basil-Infused Soda

💧 3 tablespoons **Strawberry-Basil-Infused Soda Syrup,** or to taste

8 ounces carbonated water such as club soda, seltzer, or sparkling water

Whole strawberries for garnish, if desired

To serve, spoon the Strawberry-Basil-Infused Soda Syrup into a glass, top with carbonated water, stir gently, and add ice. Another option is to spoon 1 tablespoon of syrup into a champagne flute and top with chilled sparkling wine. Taste and add more syrup, if desired.

If garnishing with whole strawberries, split each strawberry almost in half, starting at the tip and stopping as you reach the stem. Rest the split strawberry on the lip of the glass.

Erin's Tip: These recipes (pg. 86-88) are a variation on simple syrup, a combination of equal parts sugar and water. Some bartenders prefer rich simple syrup (two parts sugar to one part water) because it doesn't become as diluted in cocktails. If you plan to use your soda syrups for cocktails, you can increase the sugar, if you like.

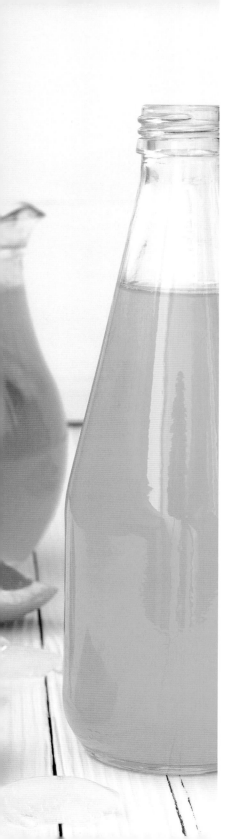

Grapefruit-Infused Soda Syrup

I always loved the taste of Squirt soda—tart, slightly bitter, and *refreshing*. I remember my dad drinking Squirt and Fresca when I was a little girl. I thought that both were grown-up drinks because they weren't as sweet as other sodas.

MAKES 2 CUPS (UP TO TEN 8-OUNCE SODAS)

> 1 cup granulated sugar
>
> 1 cup water
>
> Grated zest and juice from 2 grapefruits (I use pink grapefruit but you can use red or white if you prefer)
>
> 2 teaspoons freshly squeezed lemon juice
>
> Pinch sea salt
>
> 2 teaspoons citric acid

Combine the sugar and water in a medium saucepan along with the zest, juice, and salt. Cook over medium heat, stirring occasionally, until the sugar dissolves.

Remove the pan from the heat and allow it to cool to room temperature, about 1 hour. Strain the grapefruit syrup through a fine-mesh strainer to remove the zest and pulp. Stir in the citric acid and pour the syrup into a sterile bottle or jar.

Store the grapefruit syrup in an airtight container in the refrigerator for up to 3 weeks.

> **Erin's Tip:** I like to zest citrus with a microplane grater. No matter what you use, be sure that you only zest the very outer layer of the citrus. Too much white pith can take the soda from pleasantly bitter to sharply bitter.

▒▒ FOR THIS INFUSION, ERIN SUGGESTS MAKING ▒▒

Grapefruit Soda

> 💧 3 tablespoons **Grapefruit-Infused Soda Syrup,** or to taste
>
> 8 ounces carbonated water such as club soda, seltzer, or sparkling water

To serve, add the Grapefruit-Infused Soda Syrup to carbonated water. Enjoy over ice on a hot summer's day.

Hot Spiced Lemonade (AKA Percolator Punch)

Don't have a percolator? No problem. You can simmer the spices in a saucepan instead.

MAKES 8 SERVINGS

8 cups cold water

1 cup freshly squeezed lemon juice

30 whole cloves

1 three-inch-piece cinnamon stick or 1 teaspoon cinnamon chunks (see Resources)

4 or 5 whole allspice

1¾ cups brown sugar or honey

2-inch piece orange zest, cut with a vegetable peeler

1 lemon, sliced for garnish if desired

Place the water and lemon juice into a percolator base. Place the cloves, cinnamon, and whole allspice in the percolator basket.

Percolate for 6 to 8 minutes. For automatic percolators, simply allow the percolator to complete a standard cycle.

Place 1 tablespoon sugar into each of eight mugs. Divide the Hot Spiced Lemonade among them. Stir to incorporate the sugar. Garnish with lemon slices, if desired.

Dandelion Punch

Have a yard full of dandelions? Here's a delicious way of using them. This lightly floral punch is reminiscent of lemonade but far more delicate and refreshing.

MAKES 8 CUPS

4 cups dandelion blossoms, all green parts trimmed away

8 cups boiling water

1 orange, thinly sliced

½ lemon, thinly sliced

3 cups granulated sugar

Place dandelion blossoms in a bowl. Pour the boiling water over the blossoms, cover with a clean kitchen towel, and let steep overnight—at least 8 hours.

Pour the steeped dandelions through a fine-mesh sieve and into a large saucepan. Discard the blossoms.

Put the orange and lemon slices in a nonreactive pitcher and set aside.

Place the saucepan on the stovetop, add the sugar, and bring to a boil. Remove from the heat and carefully pour the sweetened dandelion infusion over the orange and lemon slices. Cover with a towel or piece of cheesecloth. Let stand 1 to 3 days to allow the citrus to infuse.

Strain and serve over ice. Store the remaining punch in the refrigerator for 3 to 5 days.

Watermelon & Hibiscus Agua Fresca

The tartness of the hibiscus balances the sweetness of the watermelon in this summery drink. SERVES 8 TO 10

⅔ cup dried hibiscus flowers (also called Jamaica flowers)

8 cups water

4 cups cubed ripe seedless watermelon, cut into ¾-inch dice

Agave nectar or honey, to taste, optional

Place the dried hibiscus flowers into an infusion pitcher. Add water, cover the pitcher and close the lid, and refrigerate for 8 to 12 hours. (If you don't have an infusion pitcher, you can place the flowers and water in a bowl and cover it with plastic.)

Remove the infusion tube, or strain out the blossoms. Add the watermelon cubes directly into the pitcher (not in the infusion tube). Stir and refrigerate for another 1 to 4 hours. Taste to see if you like the flavor. If you feel like it could use a touch of sweetness, add honey or agave nectar, a few tablespoons at a time, stirring to blend, until you like the flavor.

Now you have two options. You can serve the Watermelon and Hibiscus Agua Fresca with chunks of whole watermelon, or pour the mixture into a blender and purée it with some agave nectar or honey. (I use about ½ cup of agave nectar for a whole pitcher). Either way, you'll enjoy this refreshing summer quencher.

Erin's Tip: You can substitute traditional watermelon for the seedless variety. Just be sure that you've removed all the seeds if you plan to make the purée option.

What's an Agua Fresca?

Agua fresca, literally translated, means "fresh water." Common throughout Mexico, Central America, and the Caribbean, these refreshing beverages pair perfectly with spicy, rich foods. Sometimes called *aguas de frutas*, they traditionally consist of mashed fruit with just enough water to liquefy the mixture. Flowers and seeds are also used occasionally. A squeeze of lime is often added to offset the sweetness.

The key to great agua fresca is choosing fresh, ripe, seasonal fruit. Remember, the drink should be balanced—light and thirst quenching, not cloyingly sweet. Add sugar judiciously, tasting as you go. It should enhance the natural fruit, not overpower it.

Piña Colada Agua Fresca

Coconut water is low calorie and a great source of potassium. Adding pineapple punches up the fiber and vitamin C in this tropical treat. Add rum at your own risk! MAKES FOUR TO FIVE 10-OUNCE SERVINGS

1 cup fresh pineapple chunks, plus more for garnish, if desired

2 cups water

💧 1 to 2 tablespoons honey or **Ginger-Infused Honey** (page 154)

💧 ½ teaspoon **Vanilla Extract** (page 40)

2 cups coconut water

Place pineapple chunks, water, honey or Ginger-Infused Honey, and Vanilla Extract in a blender. Purée until the pineapple has liquefied.

Pour the purée into a pitcher. Stir in the coconut water. Refrigerate for a minimum of 2 hours to infuse and chill. Garnish with pineapple chunks, if desired. Serve over ice.

Pineapple, Orange & Rosemary Agua Fresca

I love the combination of the rosemary with the orange and pineapple. It's unusual but it really works! SERVES 6 TO 8

3 cups fresh pineapple chunks

1 teaspoon chopped fresh rosemary

2 tablespoons caster sugar (see page 41) or agave nectar, or to taste, optional

1 cup freshly squeezed orange juice

4 cups water

Rosemary sprigs and orange slices, for garnish

Place the pineapple chunks in a large, nonreactive bowl. Sprinkle with fresh rosemary and sugar. Stir to coat. Cover with a clean kitchen towel and let rest for 2 hours.

Scrape the pineapple and all the accumulated juices and sugar into a blender. Add the orange juice and blend until liquefied.

Strain the pineapple-orange juice through a fine-mesh strainer into a large pitcher. (This is optional. If you've blended the pineapple completely, you may not wish to strain it.)

Add the water and stir to blend. Taste the juice to see if you'd like more sugar, and adjust as needed. Refrigerate the agua fresca until completely chilled, at least 2 hours.

Serve over ice in tall glasses garnished with rosemary sprigs and orange slices, if desired.

Infused Water Variation

For a lighter version of this recipe, place 1 cup of fresh pineapple chunks in a pitcher. Slice 1 orange thinly and add to the pitcher. Toss in two 3-inch sprigs of fresh rosemary. Pour in 8 cups of water. Cover and refrigerate to infuse for 3 to 4 hours. Pour into ice-filled glasses with or without the garnish.

Mango-Basil-Infused Water

I love the flavor of mango, and basil *always* reminds me of summer. SERVES 8

1 ripe mango

8 to 10 fresh basil leaves

½ lime

8 cups water

Agave nectar or honey, to taste, optional

You can hedgehog-cut the mango (see page 31), or follow the steps below.

Use a paring knife to remove the peel from the mango. The flesh of the mango is quite slippery so be careful as you peel.

Once the peel has been removed, cut off a slice of mango from one of the long, narrow edges of the fruit—not from the stem end or tip, and not from the wide, flat side. This will allow you to stand the mango on its edge on the cutting board.

With the mango standing on its edge, slice a thick slice from one of the wide, flat sides of the fruit. Repeat until you reach the fibrous pit. Do the same on the other side. Then, lay the mango on its side and slice away as much fruit as you can from the edges without cutting into the pit.

Cut the mango slices into large chunks. Place the chunks into a pitcher or carafe.

Tear the basil leaves in half and add them to the pitcher.

Cut the lime half into wedges or chunks and add them to the pitcher. Don't squeeze; just toss the wedges into the pitcher.

Add the water. Stir to blend. Refrigerate to infuse for 2 to 3 hours.

Once the infusion is complete, pour the water over ice. You can pour the fruit and herbs into the glass as well. Or, strain the water, leaving the fruit in the pitcher and use it to make another infusion. You should be able to use the fruit for 2 additional infusions, but each infusion will take progressively more time as the fruit juices diminish. Sweeten with agave nectar or honey, if desired.

The fruit and water can be refrigerated for 1 to 2 days. That's about the maximum because the basil will begin to break down.

Agua Fresca Variation

Combine peeled and diced mango, 2 basil leaves, ½ teaspoon freshly squeezed lime juice, 1 to 2 teaspoons agave nectar or honey (or more to taste), and 1½ cups water in a blender. Purée until smooth. Refrigerate 1 hour to infuse. Strain mixture into 2 tall, ice-filled glasses and garnish with sprigs of basil. Serves 2.

Cantaloupe & Raspberry- Infused Water

Whether you want the delicate flavors of fresh melon and berries or a slightly sweeter puréed agua fresca, I've got you covered. SERVES 8 TO 10

½ ripe cantaloupe, peeled and diced (about 2 cups)

1 cup fresh raspberries

4 thin lime slices

8 cups water

Place cantaloupe, raspberries, and lime slices in an infusion pitcher or large bowl. Add water. Cover and refrigerate for 2 hours.

Serve over ice, with or without the fruit.

Agua Fresca Variation

Place diced cantaloupe and 2 cups water, 2 teaspoons freshly squeezed lime juice, and 2 teaspoons caster sugar (see page 41) in a blender. Purée until smooth. Strain mixture through a fine-mesh sieve into a pitcher. Add fresh raspberries and 2 additional cups of water. Stir to combine. Refrigerate for 1 hour to infuse flavors. Taste for additional sugar. Serve over ice. Serves 4.

Infused Oils

5

THERE ARE MANY FLAVORED OILS on the market these days. I love the diversity, but many of these oils are made with chemical flavorings instead of natural infusions. Call me crazy, but I like the real deal! Also, I'll let you in on an industry secret: many producers use lower-quality oils for flavored oil because they're going to mask the flavor anyway. The good news is you can make amazing, intensely flavorful oils yourself from natural, high-quality ingredients for a fraction of the cost.

I've included a variety of oils among the infusions. My selections were based on the combination of flavors and how I use the oil. When it comes to flavor combinations, an example might be Curry-Infused Coconut Oil. Coconut oil is used throughout Asia, so curry powder is a natural pairing. The same goes for using olive oil as the base for Pizza Drizzle Oil.

How I plan to use the oil plays a bit role in selection too. If I plan to use an oil for sautéing or other high-heat applications, I choose one with a higher smoke point such as avocado, grapeseed, sunflower, or coconut. Olive oil, on the other hand, is delicate. It's my go-to oil for salad dressings or as a finishing drizzle over the top of dishes. I know we've been trained to grab olive oil for cooking, but it really can't take much heat before it starts to smoke and oxidize. So I only use olive oil for low- to medium-heat cooking.

To help you think of more creative ways to use your infused oils, I've added several additional recipes such as Halibut Tostadas with Melon Salsa, Truffled Potato Gratin, and Mushroom Sauté with Pancetta. I also included serving suggestions at the beginning of each recipe to spark your imagination. Infused oils are a *great* way to pump up the flavor of salads, grilled and roasted vegetables, meats, seafood, and more.

Truffle-Infused Olive Oil **Pg 106**

Lemon-Infused Olive Oil

This lemon olive oil is *so* versatile. Use it to drizzle over grilled chicken or fish.
Toss with Fennel-Infused White Wine Vinegar (page 123) for a fragrant salad.
Try it in place of the Orange-Infused Olive Oil for cake (see variation below).
MAKES 1 CUP

> 2 lemons, preferably organic
>
> 1 cup mild-flavored extra-virgin olive oil

Wash the lemons under warm running water. Pat dry thoroughly. Carefully remove the peel with a vegetable peeler or channel knife (see page 120). Make sure that you aren't getting too much pith along with the zest. The pith can make the oil bitter. Reserve the lemon for another use.

Pour the olive oil into a small saucepan. Warm the oil over medium-low heat until it reaches 180° F. Add the lemon zest and continue to warm for 30 minutes. Remove the pan from the heat and cool to room temperature, approximately 1 hour.

Remove the zest using a slotted spoon. Pour the infused oil into a sterile bottle.

Store your Lemon-Infused Olive Oil in a sterile bottle or jar in the refrigerator for up to 30 days.

Olive oil becomes solid when refrigerated. Remember to take the oil out of the refrigerator about 30 minutes prior to using.

Orange-Infused Olive Oil Variation

Substitute 1 Valencia or medium navel orange for the lemons. Follow the directions as above.

Erin's Tip: Selecting organic produce is particularly important when using the peel. You don't want to introduce pesticides into your infusions.

FOR THIS INFUSION, ERIN SUGGESTS MAKING

Flatbread with Sheep's Milk Feta, Lemon-Infused Olive Oil & Mint

Feta was originally made from sheep's or goat's milk. I like the richness and tang from the sheep's-milk variety. If you can't find it, you can substitute cow's-milk feta or goat cheese. SERVES 4 AS AN ENTRÉE, OR 8 AS AN APPETIZER OR SNACK

> 4 pieces fresh or frozen flatbread (7-inch rounds)*
>
> 3 to 4 tablespoons **Lemon-Infused Olive Oil**
>
> 5 to 8 ounces sheep's-milk feta cheese or goat cheese, crumbled
>
> 2 teaspoons grated lemon zest
>
> 2 tablespoons chopped fresh mint
>
> Sea salt, to taste
>
> Crushed red pepper flakes, optional

Preheat oven to 425° F.

Place flatbread on a sheet pan. Brush the bread with a little bit of the lemon olive oil. Place the pan in the oven and bake until the bread is warm and golden, about 5 minutes for fresh or 10 for frozen.

Remove the bread from the oven and crumble the feta evenly over each piece. Bake for an additional 8 to 10 minutes, until the cheese begins to melt.

When the cheese is soft and golden, remove the bread from the oven and drizzle the remaining Lemon-Infused Olive Oil over it. Sprinkle each piece with a little lemon zest, fresh mint, salt, and crushed red pepper flakes. Cut into pieces and serve warm.

*You can substitute fresh pizza dough for the flatbread. Cut the dough into 4 to 8 pieces, stretch into ovals or rounds, and bake until golden brown. Brush with the Lemon-Infused Olive Oil and follow the remaining directions.

Lime-Infused Oil

Sautéing or grilling with lime oil is a nice way to add flavor to fish, chicken, or pork. I also love this oil combined with white balsamic vinegar for a sweet-and-sour vinaigrette—especially if I'm going to add fresh fruit to mixed greens.
MAKES 1 CUP

3 limes, preferably organic

1 cup avocado oil or grapeseed oil

Wash the limes gently under warm running water. Dry thoroughly and remove zest. I like to use a standard zester to create thin curls of zest. They infuse bright flavor but are easy to remove when you are finished infusing the oil. Be sure that you aren't getting too much white pith along with the zest. The pith can make the oil bitter.

Pour the avocado oil into a small saucepan. Add lime zest and warm over medium heat for 20 minutes.

Strain the oil through a cheesecloth-lined funnel into a small, sterile bottle. Store the oil in a sterile bottle or jar in the refrigerator for up to 30 days.

Halibut Tostadas with Melon Salsa

This recipe won a wine-and-food-pairing competition at the Culinary Institute of America in St. Helena, California. I paired it with White Hall Lane Winery's Sauvignon Blanc. MAKES 24 APPETIZERS OR 4 ENTRÉE-SIZE PORTIONS

½ honeydew melon, peeled, seeded, and finely diced

½ cup minced red onion, rinsed and drained

1 cup minced red bell pepper

½ cup chopped fresh cilantro

3 tablespoons freshly squeezed lime juice

1 tablespoon rice wine vinegar

1 teaspoon sea salt, plus extra for sprinkling

4 thin corn tortillas, each 6 inches in diameter

High-heat oil for frying

1 tablespoon **Lime-Infused Oil**

2 halibut, cod, or rockfish filets, skin removed, 6 to 8 ounces each

Sea salt and freshly ground black pepper, to taste

In a medium bowl, stir together the honeydew, red onion, red bell pepper, and cilantro. Stir in the lime juice, rice wine vinegar, and 1 teaspoon sea salt. For best flavor refrigerate at least 4 hours before serving.

To make appetizer-size tostadas, stack the tortillas in 2 equal piles. Cut each pile into 6 pie-shaped wedges, or small circles. **Note:** If you decide to cut small circles, you may need additional tortillas to make 24. If you are making full-size tostadas, simply leave the tortillas whole.

Add frying oil to a deep fryer or heavy fry pan to a depth of at least 1 inch and heat to 375° F. (That's just a touch above medium heat.) Add the tortilla pieces, a few at a time, and fry, tossing them, until golden brown. Be careful not to let them darken or they will taste bitter. Lift out and drain on paper towels. Sprinkle with sea salt while they're still hot.

Season the fish filets generously with salt and pepper. Heat the Lime-Infused Oil in a large skillet over medium-high heat.

Add the filets and sear until the fish is pale gold, about 3 to 5 minutes. Turn the filets over and cook until the flesh is opaque on the outside but still slightly translucent in the center, about 3 to 4 minutes or more, depending on the thickness of the filets. Transfer to a platter and cover loosely with aluminum foil to keep warm. When you are ready to serve, cut the filets crosswise into thin slices. Top each crisp tostada with some fish, melon salsa, and sprinkle with lime zest.

Erin's Tip: Rinsing minced or chopped onions under cool running water for a couple of minutes makes them more palatable when served raw.

Pizza Drizzle Oil

Not only is this oil *great* drizzled on pizza, but it also makes a savory addition to an Italian vinaigrette dressing. My husband loves to pour some on a small plate, sprinkle it generously with sea salt, and then dip a piece of crusty bread in it! MAKES 2¼ CUPS

1 tablespoon crushed dried fennel seeds

1 tablespoon dried oregano

2 teaspoons dried basil

2 teaspoons dried marjoram

1 teaspoon dehydrated minced garlic, or toasted minced garlic

1 teaspoon fine sea salt

¼ to ½ teaspoon crushed red pepper flakes

¼ teaspoon coarsely ground black pepper

2 cups extra-virgin olive oil

Measure the dried spices and herbs into a small saucepan. Add the olive oil and stir to combine.

Warm the oil over medium-low heat or until the temperature reaches 180°F, approximately 10 minutes. *Do not overheat the oil!* Olive oil is very delicate and will begin to break down when it is overheated.

Now pour the olive oil through the funnel into a sterile bottle or jar. You can use a toothpick or bamboo skewer to coax through any spices that get stuck in the neck of the funnel. Cap the bottle and allow it to cool to room temperature.

Store oil in the refrigerator for up to 3 months. Remember to get it out of the refrigerator about 30 minutes prior to using. Shake the bottle before each use to blend the spices.

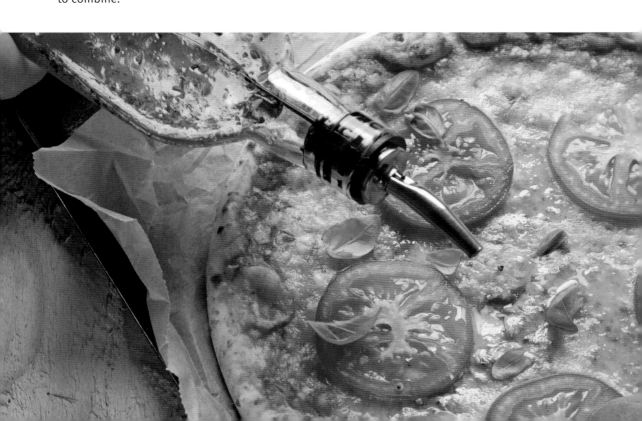

Herbes de Provence Oil

This oil is wonderful drizzled on grilled vegetables or lamb, tossed with ratatouille or roasted potatoes, or mixed into vinaigrette. MAKES JUST OVER 2 CUPS

4 teaspoons dried marjoram

1 teaspoon dried thyme

1½ teaspoons dried summer savory

½ teaspoon dried crushed rosemary

¼ teaspoon crushed dried fennel seeds

¼ teaspoon dried culinary lavender buds

Pinch dried sage

2 cups extra-virgin olive oil

Measure the dried spices and herbs into a small saucepan. Add the olive oil and stir to combine.

Warm the oil over medium-low heat or until the oil reaches 180°F, approximately 10 minutes. *Do not overheat the oil!* Olive oil is very delicate and will begin to break down when it is overheated.

Now pour the olive oil through the funnel into a sterile bottle or jar. You can use a toothpick or bamboo skewer to coax through any spices that get stuck in the neck of the funnel. Cap the bottle and allow it to cool to room temperature.

Store the oil in the refrigerator for up to 3 months. Remember to get it out of the refrigerator about 30 minutes prior to using. Shake the bottle before each use to blend the spices.

Erin's Tip: If you have an Herbes de Provence blend in your spice cupboard, you can simply add 2½ tablespoons of it in place of the dried spices listed.

What Is Herbes de Provence?

This classic French herb blend varies from person to person but traditionally includes thyme, marjoram, summer savory, rosemary, fennel seed, and other Mediterranean herbs. The addition of lavender is more recent and is sometimes left out of the mixture altogether.

Rosemary-Infused Olive Oil

Twenty years ago, I would make rosemary olive oil by adding sprigs of rosemary to oil and setting the bottle in a sunny window for a week. Crazy! Moist fresh herbs, warmth, and time create ideal conditions for growing bacteria. This method is much safer. MAKES 1 CUP

¼ cup fresh rosemary leaves, preferably organic

Pinch sea salt

1 cup extra-virgin olive oil

Wash the rosemary leaves and rinse thoroughly. Spread the clean leaves across a clean kitchen towel or a couple of layers of paper towels. Allow them to dry thoroughly, as long as overnight. Don't worry if the leaves seem to wilt slightly. When infusing oil with fresh herbs, dryness is critical.

When the leaves are dry, sprinkle them with the sea salt. Then, gather up the edges of the towel to create a pouch. While holding the towel with one hand, used your other hand to massage and bruise the leaves slightly.

Transfer the bruised leaves to a sterile, wide-mouth, pint-size Mason jar. Add the olive oil. Close the lid of the jar and shake slightly to blend. Place the jar in a cool, dark cupboard. Allow it to infuse for 1 week, shaking daily.

At the end of the week, strain the oil through a cheesecloth-lined funnel into a sterile bottle. Cap and refrigerate it until ready to use. You can store the oil for up to 3 weeks in the refrigerator. Remember to take the oil out of the refrigerator about 30 minutes prior to using.

Rosemary Caesar Salad

Rosemary complements so many of the ingredients in caesar salad—anchovies, garlic, eggs, lemon, and olive oil—it's a natural addition to the dressing.

SERVES 4 TO 6

- ½ teaspoon sea salt
- ½ teaspoon freshly ground black pepper, plus more for grinding onto the Caesar
- 1½ teaspoons garlic purée or 1 large clove of garlic, pressed
- 2 to 4 teaspoons anchovy paste
- 1 teaspoon Dijon mustard
- 2 egg yolks
- 1 teaspoon Worcestershire sauce
- 1 tablespoon white wine vinegar
- 2 tablespoons freshly squeezed lemon juice
- ⅓ cup **Rosemary-Infused Olive Oil**
- 1 large head romaine lettuce
- ⅔ cup grated **Parmigiano-Reggiano or Asiago cheese, divided**
- Garlicky croutons, optional

Measure sea salt, pepper, garlic purée, anchovy paste, and mustard into a large salad bowl. Use a fork or whisk to combine them thoroughly. Whisk in the egg yolks, Worcestershire sauce, vinegar, and lemon juice until smooth and well blended.

Add the Rosemary-Infused Olive Oil a few drops at a time, whisking constantly. After you've added a tablespoon or two by drops, you can begin to slowly stream in the remaining oil. Whisk until the oil is fully blended and the dressing is thick and smooth. Refrigerate until ready to use.

Tear the romaine leaves into bite-size pieces, and place in a large salad bowl. Add half the dressing and half of the Parmigiano-Reggiano and toss to coat. Add additional dressing if desired.

Top the salad with the remaining Parmigiano-Reggiano and a few grinds of black pepper and the croutons, if desired, and serve.

Erin's Tip: You can substitute ¼ cup of mayonnaise for the egg yolks, if you wish. Also, using real Parmigiano-Reggiano is preferable, but you can substitute Parmesan cheese instead.

Truffle-Infused Olive Oil

Truffles are incredibly expensive, so making truffle oil can extend the use of a single truffle. Truffle oil is wonderful drizzled over mashed potatoes, scrambled eggs, and risotto. You can even use it on popcorn. You'll love it on the Truffled Potato Gratin! MAKES ½ CUP

1 or 2 small white or black truffles (not quite 1½ ounce total)

½ cup mild-flavored extra-virgin olive oil

Shave paper-thin slices of the truffles using a truffle slicer or madoline. The smaller and thinner the truffle pieces, the stronger the flavor of the finished oil.

Place the truffle slices in a small saucepan with the olive oil and warm gently over *very* low heat for 1 hour. Pour the infused olive oil into a small, sterile jar. Close the jar and place it in the refrigerator for 1 week to infuse.

After the oil has infused, pour it through a fine-mesh strainer or layers of cheesecloth to remove the pieces of truffle. (You can use the truffle pieces in one of these recipe suggestions or toast some artisan bread and sprinkle it with some truffle pieces, a little of the oil, and some sea salt.)

Pour the infused oil into a sterile bottle. Cap and store in the refrigerator for up to 30 days. Remember to take the oil out of the refrigerator about 30 minutes prior to using.

Erin's Tip: Fresh truffles make the best infusion but you can use canned or frozen truffles too. It is important to understand that oil *is not* a method of preservation of truffles because there is a risk of botulism developing in the oxygen-free oil. Oil containing truffles *must be* refrigerated and used within 30 days.

Truffled Potato Gratin

Truffle oil, potatoes, cream, and fontina cheese—decadent and delicious.
Serve this dish with a good steak. SERVES 4

1 small leek

4 tablespoons room-temperature butter, divided

2 cups sliced fresh mushrooms

Sea salt and freshly ground black pepper

1 clove garlic, minced

1½ cups heavy cream

3 medium russet potatoes (about 1½ pounds), peeled and cut into ¼-inch slices

¾ cup shredded fontina cheese

1 teaspoon **Truffle-Infused Olive Oil**, or to taste

Cut off the root end and thick, dark green leaves of the leek. Slice the leek in half lengthwise. Rinse each half under cold running water, fanning the leaves slightly with your thumb so that the water gets in between the layers to flush out any grit. Pat the leek dry and slice thinly, crosswise.

Melt 3 tablespoons of butter in a medium skillet over medium heat. Add the leek and cook, stirring occasionally, until soft, about 10 minutes. Add mushrooms and sprinkle generously with salt and pepper. Increase the heat to medium-high and cook until the mushrooms have softened and the liquid evaporates, about 8 to 10 minutes. Add garlic; sauté until just fragrant, about 1 minute. Remove the pan from the heat. Taste for additional salt and pepper and add as needed. Set aside.

Preheat oven to 375° F.

In a medium saucepan, combine cream, ½ teaspoon sea salt, and ¼ teaspoon black pepper. Add potatoes. (The potatoes won't be completely covered by the cream.) Bring to a boil over medium-high heat, then reduce heat to medium, cover, and simmer 10 minutes, stirring occasionally.

Remove lid; simmer until cream has thickened slightly and potatoes are partially cooked, about 3 minutes. Stir often while the cream is thickening to prevent the mixture from scorching.

Use the remaining 1 tablespoon of butter to grease a small baking dish or gratin pan. Use a slotted spoon to scoop about half the potatoes into the buttered dish. Spread the mushrooms and leeks evenly over the potatoes. Layer the remaining potatoes over the mushrooms and leeks. Pour the cream over the top. Sprinkle with the fontina cheese.

Cover and bake for 30 minutes. Uncover and bake 10 to 15 minutes longer or until potatoes are lightly browned. Let potatoes rest for 10 minutes before serving. Drizzle with the Truffle-Infused Olive Oil, top with a few grinds of black pepper, and serve.

Erin's Tip: You can use whatever mushrooms you like. I used cremini, but a combination of wild mushrooms would be delicious as well.

Wild-Mushroom & Sage-Infused Olive Oil

I used Spice Jungle's Northwoods Mushroom Blend—a combination of lobster, shiitake, porcini, oyster, morel, and bolete mushrooms—a super-earthy, delicious blend. This infused oil makes a great finishing drizzle for steaks, pork chops, and even halibut. MAKES 2 CUPS

1 ounce dried mushrooms

2 cups extra-virgin olive oil

1 tablespoon dried whole sage leaves

Place the mushrooms in a medium saucepan. Add the oil and sage. Stir to combine.

Heat the oil over medium heat until it reaches 180°F, approximately 5 minutes. *Do not overheat the oil!*

Pour the mushroom oil into a wide-mouth, quart Mason jar. Cover and place in a dark location to infuse for 2 to 3 weeks.

At the end of the infusion time, strain the infused oil through several layers of cheesecloth to remove the mushrooms. (See Erin's Tip.)

Pour the strained oil into a sterile bottle. Cap and store in the refrigerator for up to 30 days. Remember to take the oil out of the refrigerator about 30 minutes prior to using.

Erin's Tip: If you plan to make the Mushroom Sauté with Pancetta, place the mushrooms into a small bowl. Add boiling water to cover and let the mushrooms soak for 45 minutes.

Mushroom Sauté with Pancetta

Use your favorite mushrooms for this recipe—whatever is in season. I like to use a blend of cremini, stemmed shiitakes, and oyster mushrooms. SERVES 4 TO 6

1 ounce dried mushrooms, your choice

4 ounces diced pancetta

¼ cup minced shallots

1 tablespoon clarified butter or ghee

1 pound assorted fresh mushrooms, your choice, cut into large pieces

½ teaspoon dried thyme

2 teaspoons minced fresh sage, or 1 teaspoon dried

2 to 3 cloves garlic, sliced

⅓ cup dry sherry or dry white wine

1 tablespoon Wild-Mushroom & Sage-Infused Olive Oil

Sea salt and freshly ground black pepper, to taste

Place the dried mushrooms into a medium bowl. Add boiling water to cover and let the mushrooms soak for 45 minutes. Remove the mushrooms from the bowl with a slotted spoon. Strain the liquid through several layers of cheesecloth to remove any debris or sediment. Reserve the liquid. (See Erin's Tip.)

Warm a large skillet over medium heat. Add the pancetta, reduce the heat to medium-low, and cook until most of the fat has been rendered and the pancetta is just beginning to crisp, about 10 minutes. Stir in the shallots and continue to cook until the shallots are slightly translucent, about 1 to 2 minutes. Use a slotted spoon to remove the shallots and pancetta. Set aside.

Increase the heat to medium-high, add the ghee to the pan. After the ghee has melted, stir in the fresh mushrooms, thyme, and sage. Sprinkle with ½ teaspoon of salt and sauté until the mushrooms have browned and all the liquid has evaporated, about 10 minutes. Stir in the reconstituted dried mushrooms and garlic. Cook for 1 to 2 minutes longer.

Return the pancetta and shallots to the pan. Add the sherry and cook until the wine evaporates, about 4 to 5 minutes.

Remove the pan from the heat, stir in the Wild-Mushroom & Sage-Infused Olive Oil. Season to taste with salt and pepper and serve.

Erin's Tip: You may use the reserved mushroom liquid in place of the sherry, if you wish.

Curry-Infused Coconut Oil

This oil is so good for stir-fried vegetables. You can also melt it and toss it with cauliflower florets just prior to roasting them. MAKES ½ CUP

½ cup coconut oil

4 teaspoons sweet curry powder

Measure the coconut oil into a small saucepan. Cook the oil over medium-low heat until it has melted to its liquid form, about 5 minutes. Add the curry powder and stir to combine.

Remove the pan from the heat. Cover and infuse for 30 minutes. The oil should still be liquid.

Use a rubber scraper to coax the curry oil into a sterile, wide-mouth, half-pint Mason jar. Since the oil will be solid again after it's cooled completely, storing it in a wide-mouth jar makes it much easier to use.

Store, covered, in the refrigerator for up to 30 days. It's a good idea to take the oil out of the refrigerator at least 30 minutes prior to using for cooking. This allows the oil to soften slightly so you can spoon it out of the jar.

Mustard-Infused Oil

This spicy oil is great tossed with roasted red potatoes or cauliflower. You can also use it to spoon over roasted chicken or fish. MAKES ¼ CUP

1 tablespoon ground mustard

¼ teaspoon cayenne pepper

¼ teaspoon ground turmeric, optional

¼ teaspoon salt

2 tablespoons water

¼ cup sunflower or safflower oil

¼ teaspoon whole brown mustard seeds

¼ teaspoon whole cumin seeds

¼ teaspoon whole fennel seeds

Sea salt, to taste

Combine ground mustard, cayenne pepper, turmeric (if using), and salt in a small prep bowl. Mix with a fork to blend.

Place water in another small bowl. Slowly add the mustard spice blend, whisking constantly with a fork until you have a thick paste. Set aside.

Pour the oil into a small skillet or saucepan and set over medium-high heat. When hot, add the brown mustard seeds. They will start to pop almost immediately. As soon as they do, add the cumin and fennel seeds and remove the pan from the heat. Stir once, and quickly pour the hot oil into the mustard paste. Use the fork to whisk the mixture until well blended.

Cover with plastic wrap and let the mixture infuse at room temperature for several hours or as long as overnight. The longer the Mustard-Infused Oil stands at room temperature, the milder it will become.

Season with salt. Pour the seasoned oil into a sterile bottle or jar. Cap and store in the refrigerator for up to 30 days. Remember to take the oil out of the refrigerator about 30 minutes prior to using.

Smoked Paprika & Cumin-Infused Olive Oil

If I were a spice, I'd be Spanish *pimentón*—surprising, a little exotic, and spicy. Okay, so there's nothing exotic about me, but I still *love* this infused oil! MAKES ½ CUP

½ teaspoon whole cumin seeds

½ cup extra-virgin olive oil

1 tablespoon mild Spanish pimentón (smoked paprika)

Place the cumin seeds in a small, dry skillet over medium-high heat. Toast until quite fragrant, about 30 seconds to 1 minute, depending out how quickly the pan heats. Transfer the toasted seeds to a mortar and pestle or spice grinder and grind to a powder. Set aside.

In a small saucepan, heat the olive oil over medium-low heat until the oil is lukewarm. Don't overheat the oil or it can become bitter. Whisk in the ground cumin and pimentón. When the spices are thoroughly blended, remove the pan from the heat and allow the spices to steep as the oil cools to room temperature.

Transfer the cooled oil to a sterilized container, cover, and store in the refrigerator for up to 1 week. Remember to take the oil out of the refrigerator about 30 minutes prior to using. The spices can float to the top of the oil, so mix well before using.

Not Yo' Mama's Paprika! (Unless You're from Spain)

When I was growing up we used paprika in one of two ways: as a garnish on potato salad or deviled eggs, and in chicken paprikash (because of my Hungarian ancestry). Beyond that, paprika simply sat in the spice rack. I suppose that's the way most of you think of paprika too. It's kind of just for color. Well, no more!

When I was in culinary school I discovered Spanish smoked paprika, called *pimentón*. It changed the way I think about paprika forever.

The best pimentón comes from an area called La Vera Valley in Spain. It's not so much the growing of the peppers in La Vera, but what they do at harvest that makes it the best. In the fall, pepper varieties are handpicked and smoked in small smokehouses near the fields. The smokehouses are simple structures with concrete floors. Wooden grates are suspended several feet above the floors over smoldering oak fires. The peppers are dried over the smoke for 10 to 15 days. The smoking process imparts a deep, rich, smoky aroma that you don't get from typical grocery-store-brand paprika.

Pimentón is a staple of Spanish cooking. It's used in sausages, *papas bravas* (spicy, fried potatoes), garlic shrimp, and other tapas dishes, as well as stews, paella, and sauces.

Spanish pimentón comes in three styles: *dulce* (literally meaning sweet, but more accurately mild), *agrodulce* (bittersweet or slightly spicy), and *picante* (spicy hot). The flavor is amazing. There's a depth to it—layers of smoky, dusty, peppery flavors—and depending on the style, heat and spice.

You can find pimentón at specialty grocers or on-line. Try to purchase pimentón de la Vera to ensure you're getting good quality and flavor. Go ahead, give it a try. You'll never think of paprika the same way again.

Lentil Salad with Smoked Paprika & Cumin-Infused Olive Oil

For salads, I like to use black caviar lentils or French lentils (also called le Puy lentils), because they hold their shape. If you can't find black or French lentils, you can substitute brown lentils, but reduce the cooking time by 5 to 7 minutes.

SERVES 4 TO 6

1 cup black caviar or French lentils, rinsed and picked over

2 cloves garlic

1 dried bay leaf

1¼ teaspoon sea salt, divided

4 teaspoons sherry vinegar or red wine vinegar

Pinch cayenne pepper

¼ cup **Smoked Paprika & Cumin-Infused Olive Oil**

1 medium carrot, peeled and grated

1 green onion, thinly sliced

½ cup finely diced red bell pepper

2 tablespoons chopped fresh parsley

½ cup crumbled feta cheese

¼ teaspoon ground cumin

Freshly ground black pepper, to taste

Place the lentils in a medium saucepan with the garlic and bay leaf. Add enough water to cover the lentils by 2 inches. Bring the water to a boil. Reduce the heat and simmer for 20 minutes. Add ½ teaspoon sea salt and continue to cook until the lentils are tender, about 5 more minutes. Try not to overcook the lentils or they'll become mushy. Drain the lentils through a colander and rinse under cold running water to stop the cooking process. Transfer to a bowl.

In a small bowl, whisk together the sherry vinegar, the remaining ¾ teaspoon salt, and cayenne until the salt dissolves. Slowly whisk in the Smoked-Paprika-and-Cumin-Infused Olive Oil.

Stir half of the dressing into the warm lentils and refrigerate for 20 minutes.

Add the carrot, green onions, bell pepper, parsley, and remaining dressing to the lentils, and stir to combine. Top with the feta cheese, ground cumin, and freshly ground black pepper. Serve at room temperature.

Vinegars & Gastriques

6

INFUSED VINEGAR is one of the best-kept secrets of true salad dressing aficionados. From fresh herbs to fruit and aromatic spices, the combinations are limitless. You can create myriad flavors that require little beyond good oil to make delectable salad dressings in a snap.

I wanted to experiment with different flavors for this chapter, so along with wine and cider vinegars, I've included a few lesser-known vinegars such as coconut vinegar, rice vinegar, and white balsamic. I also added a recipe for homemade cider vinegar, an infusion of sweetened water and fresh apples, just for fun.

Almost anything makes a good vinegar infusion, from fruits and vegetables to herbs and aromatic spices. Vinegar is also easy to infuse because of its acidic nature. Plus, it stores well—usually 6 months to 1 year.

Many of us don't think about vinegar beyond salad dressings and pickles. To change things up, I threw in a few *gastrique* recipes. A gastrique is a simple sweet-and-sour sauce. It can be used on its own or as part of another sauce. You're going to *love* the Duck Breasts with Cherry Gastrique, and the Broiled Apricots with Lemon Verbena Gastrique are simply to die for.

If you think vinegar is an incidental condiment, I hope you are pleasantly surprised!

Lemongrass-Infused Rice Vinegar **Pg 122**

Apple Cider Vinegar

Try a blend of tart and sweet apples to create balance. I like the combination of 4 Granny Smiths and 8 Galas, but you should experiment with other apples too.

MAKES 4 TO 5 CUPS

12 small to medium apples, preferably organic

1 cup turbinado sugar or granulated sugar

4 cups water or more as needed, divided

Thoroughly wash and chop the apples into medium-size pieces. You may include the skin, cores, and seeds, but toss out the stems. Place the chopped apples in a sterile, wide-mouth, ½-gallon Mason jar or crock.

Place the sugar and 1 cup of water in a medium saucepan. Warm the water over medium, low heat, stirring occasionally, until the sugar dissolves, about 5 minutes. Stir in the remaining 3 cups of water.

Pour the sugar water over the apples. Add more room-temperature water, as needed, to cover the apples.

Cut a double-layer, 8 x 8-inch square of cheesecloth. Place it over the mouth of the jar and secure it with kitchen twine or a large rubber band.

Place the jar in a warm location, away from direct sunlight, for 1 to 3 weeks. Mix gently with a wooden spoon, once a day. When you start to notice bubbles forming and the apple scraps/chunks no longer float, it's time to strain the cider. The length of time will depend on the warmth of the environment.

Strain the liquid through a fine-mesh strainer. Discard the apple pieces. Pour the strained liquid into a fresh, sterile, half-gallon Mason jar or crock. Cover it with a fresh double layer of cheesecloth and secure as before.

Return the jar to the same warm place and for roughly 4 to 6 weeks. You may see sediment forming at the bottom of the jar; this is normal. A culture similar to a kombucha SCOBY (see page 72) should form on the top of the liquid. It will be cloudy but should show no sign of mold growth.

After 4 weeks, taste the vinegar. If it has reached a good level of acidity—meaning it tastes sharp like vinegar and you are satisfied with the flavor—you can strain it through several layers of cheesecloth into a saucepan. You can use this vinegar mother to start a new batch of cider vinegar. Using the mother will speed the fermentation process.

Place the saucepan over medium heat. Warm the vinegar to 140°F but no more than 150°F. You can use a candy thermometer to determine the temperature. Warming the vinegar to 140°F pasteurizes the vinegar and stops the fermentation process.* Continue cooking at this temperature for 30 minutes.

Funnel the warm Apple Cider Vinegar into a sterile bottle. Store at room temperature away from direct sunlight.

*Note: Some people prefer raw vinegar, which is quite healthful but has a shorter shelf life. Pasteurized vinegar can be stored almost indefinitely.

FOR THIS INFUSION, ERIN SUGGESTS MAKING

Spiced Cider Vinegar

Spiced Cider Vinegar makes flavorful vinaigrettes for autumn salads. I love to use it on salads of hearty winter greens, dried fruits and nuts, fresh apples or pears, and tangy cheeses. MAKES 2 CUPS

1½ teaspoons whole cloves

1½ teaspoons whole allspice

1 three-inch-piece cinnamon stick

½ teaspoon dried sweet orange peel or 1-inch strip orange zest, cut with a vegetable peeler for a wide strip

2 cups **Apple Cider Vinegar** or good-quality commercial cider vinegar

Place spices and orange zest in a sterile, wide-mouth, pint Mason jar or small crock. Add the Apple Cider Vinegar. Close the jar and shake to blend the contents.

Store the jar in cool, dark cupboard for 4 weeks. Shake the jar 3 or 4 times a week. Taste occasionally to check the vinegar's flavor.

When the flavor is to your liking, strain the Spiced Cider Vinegar through a cheesecloth-lined funnel into a sterile bottle. Cork and store in a cool, dark place for up to 6 months.

Ginger-Infused Coconut Vinegar

Coconut vinegar is made from fermented coconut water (from the coconuts) or from the sap and blossoms of the coconut tree, depending on the producer. Used throughout the Philippines and parts of India, coconut vinegar is high in potassium and amino acids. You can substitute it for apple cider vinegar in many recipes. MAKES 2 CUPS

1 two-inch piece fresh ginger (about 2 ounces)

2 cups coconut vinegar

Peel the ginger using a teaspoon or vegetable peeler. Mince or grate the ginger.

Place a funnel in the neck of a sterile bottle. Feed the ginger through the funnel into the bottle. Tap or shake the funnel to encourage the ginger to slide through. If you find that the ginger is clogging the neck of the funnel, use a toothpick or bamboo skewer to push it through. Don't worry if you can't loosen all the ginger from the funnel, the vinegar will wash it down.

Pour the coconut vinegar through the funnel into the bottle. Cap the bottle tightly and invert it to blend the ginger. Place the bottle on your counter or in a cupboard to infuse for 1 week. Shake or invert the bottle daily.

At the end of the infusion, strain the vinegar through a fine-mesh strainer or cheesecloth to remove the ginger. Funnel the vinegar into a sterile bottle and store, capped, in a cool, dry location for up to 6 months.

If you notice that the strength of the ginger begins to dissipate over time, you can add a few teaspoons of fresh minced ginger to perk up the flavor.

Summer Rolls with Ginger-Sesame Dipping Sauce

Be sure the vegetables are cut into very fine matchsticks or fine julienne. If they're too big, they'll be bulky and difficult to wrap and may tear the delicate wrappers. The easiest way to accomplish this is by using a mandoline.

MAKES 8 ROLLS

- ¼ cup plus 2 tablespoons **Ginger-Infused Coconut Vinegar**, divided
- 1 tablespoon tamari or regular soy sauce
- ½ teaspoon garlic purée or 1 large clove of garlic, pressed
- 1 tablespoon honey
- 1 teaspoon sesame oil
- ½ teaspoon sriracha sauce, optional
- 2 ounces rice vermicelli noodles or bean thread noodles
- 12 medium shrimp, cooked, peeled, and deveined
- 16 to 24 fresh mint leaves
- 16 fresh Thai basil or regular basil leaves
- 1 ripe mango, peeled and thinly slivered
- 1 medium hothouse cucumber, matchstick cut (fine julienne)
- 1 medium red bell pepper, matchstick cut (fine julienne)
- 8 eight-inch rice-paper rounds

To make the Ginger-Sesame Dipping Sauce, place ¼ cup Ginger-Infused Coconut Vinegar, tamari, garlic purée, honey, sesame oil, and sriracha, if using, in a small bowl. Whisk until blended. Set aside.

Cook the noodles according to the package. Rinse with cold water to chill. Drain thoroughly. Transfer the cold, drained noodles to a bowl and toss with 2 tablespoons Ginger-Infused Coconut Vinegar. Set aside.

Lay the shrimp on a cutting board. Place your knife parallel to the cutting board and slice each shrimp in half lengthwise so you have two mirror-image halves. Cover and refrigerate until ready to use.

Line up your ingredients in front of you like an assembly line, left to right. Start with the shrimp on the left, followed by cooked noodles, mint, basil, mango, cucumber, and bell pepper.

Fill a large ceramic baking dish with warm water. Dip a rice paper round into the water. A quick dip of about 2 seconds is plenty. Place the rice paper round on a clean work surface and pat gently with a paper towel or clean kitchen towel.

Line up 3 shrimp halves in the center of the rice paper with the outside of the shrimp facing down. Top the shrimp with a little bit of rice noodles, 2 to 3 mint leaves, 2 basil leaves, a couple slivers of mango, and a few sticks of cucumber and bell pepper. Be careful not to overstuff, or it will be difficult to roll the wrapper.

Fold the bottom edge of each round over the filling. Snug the filling slightly with the wrapper, and then fold in the ends. Finish by rolling up the rice paper rounds tightly to enclose the filling. Transfer the rolls to the platter. Repeat with remaining rice paper rounds.

Cover with a slightly damp paper towel, then plastic wrap; chill. You can make your summer rolls up to 8 hours ahead of time. Just make sure they are well wrapped so they don't dry out. Serve rolls with Ginger-Sesame Dipping Sauce.

Lemon-Dill-Infused Vinegar

Lemon and dill are natural companions. This bright, fragrant vinegar is very nice for a simple vinaigrette. I also like it in German or Scandinavian potato salads, but my favorite use is the Lemon-Dill Cucumber Salad. MAKES 2 CUPS

1 large lemon, preferably organic

1 small bunch fresh dill (about 10–15 sprigs)

2 cups good-quality champagne or white wine vinegar

Wash the lemon under warm running water. Pat dry thoroughly. Remove the peel using a channel knife so that you create long, pretty curls of zest (see Erin's Tip). Alternatively, you can use a vegetable peeler to remove wider strips of zest. As always, try not to get too much pith along with the zest.

Wash the fresh dill and pat it dry.

Place the lemon zest and dill sprigs into a sterile bottle or wide-mouth quart-sized Mason jar. Since zest and herbs are pickled during the infusion, there is no need to remove them at the end. If you'd rather remove the ingredients when the infusion is complete, a wide-mouth jar is your best option. Secure the lid and place the container in a cool, dark location for 3 weeks. Shake the container every few days to increase the infusion.

Erin's Tip: A channel knife is a tool used for garnishing. Bartenders usually have one on hand to make fruit twists for cocktails. My favorite is made by a company called Messermeister (German for "knife master").

Lemon-Dill Cucumber Salad

You could just as well call it "Tangy, Herbaceous, and Refreshing Salad"! SERVES 6

2 hothouse/English cucumbers

2 teaspoons sea salt

½ cup thinly sliced red onion

2 tablespoons **Lemon-Dill Infused Vinegar** (page 120)

2 teaspoons caster sugar (page 41)

6 tablespoons extra-virgin olive oil or Lemon-Infused Olive Oil (page 98)

1 teaspoon freshly grated lemon zest

¼ cup chopped fresh dill

Freshly ground black pepper, to taste

Wash, pat dry, and thinly slice both cucumbers—the thinner the better. We're talking ¹⁄₁₆-inch slices. If you have a mandoline, it will cut the slicing time in half.

Place the cucumbers in a colander. Sprinkle with salt and toss to coat. Place the colander in the sink or over a bowl. Allow the cucumbers to drain for 30 minutes.

While the cucumbers are resting, place the red onion slices in a colander or sieve and rinse under cold running water for 1 to 2 minutes. Drain and set aside.

Lightly rinse the cucumber slices under cold running water. Transfer the slices to a clean kitchen towel. Gather the edges, twist and squeeze to remove as much moisture from the cucumbers as possible. Set these aside while you mix the dressing.

Measure the Lemon-Dill Infused Vinegar into a large bowl and whisk in the sugar until it dissolves in the vinegar. Slowly whisk in the olive oil. Add the lemon zest, and stir to blend.

Mix in the cucumbers, sliced onions, and fresh dill, and toss to coat with the dressing. Let the salad marinate in the refrigerator for 1 hour until fully chilled. Taste to see if it needs additional salt. Season with a few grinds of black pepper, and serve.

Lemongrass-Infused Rice Vinegar

See photo Pg 115. Lemongrass is quite fibrous, so you need to beat it up a little to get the most flavor in your infusion. MAKES 1½ CUPS

3 stalks fresh lemongrass

1½ cups unseasoned rice wine vinegar, preferably organic

1 teaspoon granulated cane sugar, optional

Wash the lemongrass stalks and pat dry. Peel away the drier outer leaves. Trim off the root of the stalks, then cut away any green leaves so that you're left with the white and pale yellow center of the stalk. (If you purchased a trimmed stalk, you may not have any green leaves to deal with.) Cut the center stalks into 2- to 3-inch sections.

Use a mallet, rolling pin, or a heavy saucepan to smash the lemongrass stalks pieces. This helps to release the essential oils. Next, cut the lemongrass into rings, about ½ inch thick.

Place the rings into a sterile, wide-mouth, pint-sized Mason jar.

Pour the rice wine vinegar into a nonreactive saucepan. Add the sugar, if using. Cook over medium heat until it is just below a simmer, about 5 minutes. Stir to blend the sugar.

Pour the warm vinegar over the lemongrass rings. Close the lid tightly. Place the jar in a cool, dark location and allow the vinegar to infuse for 2 to 3 weeks. Shake the jar occasionally to maximize the infusion.

Strain the Lemongrass-Infused Rice Vinegar through a fine-mesh sieve to remove the lemongrass stalks. Store in a cool, dark location in a sterile jar or bottle with a tight-fitting lid for up to 1 year.

Erin's Tip: When purchasing lemongrass, try to find fresh-looking stalks that are free of brownish blemishes. Lemongrass is often sold pretrimmed in plastic clamshell containers too. Check for freshness by looking at the cut ends. They shouldn't look brown or dry.

Fennel-Infused White Wine Vinegar

This vinegar is one of my favorites—simple and full of flavor. It makes a *fabulous* vinaigrette. Try a simple salad of butter lettuce, radicchio, carrot curls, shaved raw fennel, Fennel-Infused White Wine Vinegar, olive oil, salt, and pepper. MAKES 1½ CUPS

1 small fennel bulb with fronds intact

1½ cups good-quality white wine vinegar

Thoroughly rinse the fennel and pat it dry with paper towels or a clean kitchen towel. Break off the delicate fronds and set aside. Cut the woody stalks off the bulb and discard. Slice the bulb, crosswise, as thinly as possible. You should have about 1½ cups of sliced fennel.

Place the sliced fennel and fronds into a sterile, wide-mouth, quart Mason jar.

Pour the vinegar over the fennel. If the fennel is not fully submerged, press it down with a wooden spoon or remove a couple of slices from the jar. Close the lid securely. Allow the vinegar to infuse in a cool, dark place, undisturbed, for 3 to 4 weeks.

Strain the Fennel-Infused White Wine Vinegar through a cheesecloth-lined, fine-mesh sieve into a sterile jar or bottle. Discard the fennel slices and fronds.

Store in a cool, dark location for up to 1 year.

Pear-Infused White Balsamic Vinegar

This delicate, fruity vinegar is wonderful on any salad with fruit. MAKES 1½ CUPS

1 cup diced pears (1 large), Bosc, Concorde, or Seckel pears work well

1½ cups good-quality white balsamic vinegar

Wash, peel, and dice the pears. Discard the peels, seeds, and stems. Place the diced pears in a sterile, wide-mouth, quart-sized Mason jar.

Pour the vinegar over the pears. Close the lid and place it in a dark cupboard for at least 2 weeks. Normally, I suggest shaking the vinegar to enhance vinegar to fruit contact, but to keep this vinegar clear and sparkling, I don't recommend shaking. Time will give you plenty of infusion flavor.

The infusion can take as long as 6 weeks, depending on the strength of flavor you prefer. Begin to taste the vinegar at 2 weeks. If you are satisfied with the flavor, you can strain the liquid into a sterile bottle.

To get the clearest vinegar, dampen several layers of cheesecloth with a little water. Squeeze to remove the excess water. Use the damp cheesecloth to line a funnel, and pour the infused vinegar through the funnel into a sterile bottle or jar.

You can store the Pear-Infused White Balsamic Vinegar in a cool dark place for 2 to 3 months, or for up to 8 months in the refrigerator.

Erin's Tip: White balsamic vinegar is a combination of the pressings ("must") of Trebbiano grapes and white wine vinegar. It has a similar flavor to traditional balsamic, but is a little less sweet.

Pear Profiles

The **Comice Pear** is lightly sweet and earthy. It makes an excellent companion for soft, creamy cheese.

Try the mellow and juicy **Green Anjou** raw, poached, or roasted.

The traditional soft-green **Bartlett Pear** is the classic canning pear. When you imagine a ripe, juicy pear, it's probably a Bartlett.

The bright-green **Concorde Pear** is sweet with hints of vanilla. This pear is good for salads, since it doesn't brown as quickly as other pears.

The firm, golden-brown **Bosc Pear** has bold flavor that can be a bit musty. The texture lends itself to roasting and poaching.

Arugula Salad with Pears & Gorgonzola

I like the peppery flavor of arugula. Balancing it with the sweetness of pear and the saltiness of gorgonzola makes a fabulous salad. Diced roasted beets are also a nice addition to this salad. SERVES 4

- 1 ripe pear, Concorde or Bosc are my favorites
- 2 tablespoons **Pear-Infused White Balsamic Vinegar**
- 2 tablespoons walnut oil or extra-virgin olive oil, or a combination
- 1 teaspoon finely minced shallot or ¼ teaspoon granulated onion
- 5 ounces baby arugula
- ½ cup crumbled gorgonzola
- ¼ cup toasted walnut pieces
- Sea salt and freshly ground black pepper

Wash the dry the pear. Cut the pear into lengthwise quarters. Carefully core each quarter with a paring knife. Slice each quarter into thin lengthwise slices or dice it if you prefer. If you are not planning to prepare the salad immediately, place the pear pieces into a bowl of cool water with a squeeze of lemon and a pinch of salt. Remove the pear pieces from the lemon water and pat dry before placing them on the salad.

Measure the Pear-Infused White Balsamic Vinegar, oil, and shallot into a large salad bowl. Whisk to combine. Add the arugula, and toss to coat. Season liberally with salt and pepper.

Divide the greens between 4 salad plates. Top with pieces of pear. Divide the gorgonzola evenly among the 4 salads. Top with toasted walnuts. Season to taste with additional sea salt and freshly ground black pepper. Serve immediately.

Fig-Infused Balsamic Vinegar

Fig-infused balsamic makes a great vinaigrette dressing for late-summer salads with arugula, fresh figs or apples, walnuts, and salty cheeses such as feta or *ricotta salata.* MAKES 3 CUPS

1 cup stemmed, coarsely chopped dried black mission figs

2 cups good-quality balsamic vinegar

1 sprig fresh rosemary, optional

Place the figs in a nonreactive saucepan and pour the balsamic vinegar over them.

Heat the saucepan over medium heat until the vinegar begins to simmer. Remove the pan from the heat and drop in the rosemary sprig, if using. Cover the pan and allow the figs to steep for 2 hours.

Remove the rosemary sprig. Pour the infused vinegar into a sterile, wide-mouth bottle or jar so that the fig pieces can move freely. Alternatively, you can pour the entire mixture into a blender and purée until it is smooth. I'm a bit partial to the fig chunks, myself.

The vinegar will keep in the refrigerator for up to 3 months. Shake before each use.

FOR THIS INFUSION, ERIN SUGGESTS MAKING

Grilled-Eggplant Salad with Fig-Infused Balsamic Vinaigrette

This luscious salad has Mediterranean roots. I love the sweet-savory combination of the fig balsamic with the vegetables and salty cheese. SERVES 6 TO 8

1 cup **Fig-Infused Balsamic Vinegar** with fig pieces

⅓ cup extra-virgin olive oil

2 medium eggplants (about 1 pound each), sliced to ½-inch thick, lengthwise

1 jumbo sweet onion, such as Vidalia or Walla Walla

2 medium red bell peppers

¾ cup safflower or sunflower oil, or other high-heat oil

2 teaspoons chopped fresh rosemary

2 teaspoons chopped fresh mint or marjoram

1 cup crumbled feta or *ricotta salata*

Sea salt and freshly ground black pepper, to taste

Preheat grill to medium.

Place the Fig-Infused Balsamic Vinegar in a small, nonreactive saucepan over high heat.

Cook until reduced by half, 5 minutes. Remove from heat, stir in the olive oil, and let cool.

Place the eggplant slices on a large, rimmed sheet pan.

Slice the onion into ½-inch-thick crosswise slices. Secure each slice with a skewer or toothpicks so the rings stay together. Add the onion slices to the large, rimmed sheet pan.

Remove the stems and seeds from the bell peppers and slice each pepper into 8 lengthwise strips. Add the peppers to the sheet pan with the eggplant and onions.

Drizzle or brush the vegetables on both sides with safflower oil until evenly coated. Grill the vegetables, covered, until slightly charred and tender, about 4 minutes per side.

Place the vegetables on a large platter. Sprinkle generously with sea salt, pepper, rosemary, and mint or marjoram. Top with crumbled feta. Drizzle with the cooled vinegar mixture. Serve.

Blueberry-Infused Gastrique

The combination of blueberries and cinnamon is delicious. You can serve this gastrique over vanilla ice cream as well as alongside Pork Loin Medallions (see recipe). MAKES ABOUT 1½ CUPS

½ cup honey

½ cup brown sugar

1 cup good-quality red wine vinegar

2 cups blueberries, fresh or frozen

1 cinnamon stick

Place the honey, brown sugar, red wine vinegar, and blueberries in a medium saucepan. Bring the mixture to a boil over medium-high heat. Reduce heat slightly, and simmer until the liquid has reduced by two-thirds. The gastrique should be syrupy.

Remove the pan from the heat. Add the cinnamon stick, cover, and allow to infuse for 30 minutes.

Remove the cinnamon stick, and serve.

Pork Loin Medallions with Blueberry-Infused Gastrique

The key to juicy, delicious pork is brining. Oh—and a fabulous sauce such as this one! SERVES 4

1 quart cool water

Scant ½ cup kosher salt

¼ cup granulated sugar

¼ cup brown sugar

2 bay leaves

¼ teaspoon whole allspice

6 whole black peppercorns

1 pork tenderloin, about ½ pound

1 to 2 tablespoons high-heat oil such as sunflower or safflower oil

💧 **Blueberry-Infused Gastrique**, warmed, for drizzling

Combine the water, salt, sugars, bay leaves, allspice, and peppercorns in a large saucepan. Cook over medium-low heat, stirring constantly, until the sugars dissolve. Remove the saucepan from the heat, and place the brine solution in the refrigerator to cool.

When the brine is completely cool, add the pork tenderloin. You can brine the tenderloin in the same pan that you used for the brine solution. I usually place a small plate on top of the tenderloin to keep it submerged. You can also place the tenderloin in a gallon Ziploc bag and fill it with the brine solution. Close the bag securely to avoid leaks. Brine the tenderloin for 1 hour.

After 1 hour, remove the tenderloin from the solution and pat it dry with paper towels. Slice the tenderloin into twelve 1-inch slices.

Heat 1 tablespoon oil in a large, heavy skillet over medium-high heat. Add the pork medallions and sauté for about 1½ to 2 minutes per side. The medallions should be nicely browned and the internal temperature should be between 140°F to 145°F.

Remove the medallions to a platter or individual plates, loosely tent with aluminum foil, and let rest for 5 minutes. Spoon or drizzle with the Blueberry-Infused Gastrique, and serve.

Erin's Tip: When brining, a good rule of thumb is 1 hour of brining per pound of meat with a 1 hour minimum and 12 hours maximum.

Cherry-Infused Balsamic Gastrique

A little bit of sweet-and-sour heaven! MAKES ABOUT 1 CUP

¾ cup granulated sugar

¼ cup water

1 cup good-quality balsamic vinegar

5 whole cloves

1½ cups pitted dark sweet cherries, fresh or frozen

Place the granulated sugar and water in a medium saucepan. Stir to combine. Cook over medium-high heat until the sugar caramelizes and becomes amber colored, about 3 to 5 minutes. *Do not stir* while the sugar is caramelizing. Just let it bubble and brown in the pan.

When the sugar becomes a rich amber color, stir in the vinegar. The sugar will bubble and sputter but don't be alarmed, just keep stirring until the vinegar and sugar combine to become syrup-like. Stir in the cloves. Continue to cook until the sugared vinegar has reduced by about half, about 3 to 5 minutes.

Cover the pan, remove from the heat, and infuse for 15 to 30 minutes.

Remove the cloves. Return the pan to the stovetop over medium heat, and add the cherries. Bring the *gastrique* to a simmer, cover, and cook until the cherries have softened and begun to release their juices, about 5 minutes. Serve with Pan-Seared Duck Breasts (see recipe).

Pan-Seared Duck Breast with Cherry-Infused Balsamic Gastrique

Duck and cherries is a classic combination. The tartness of the gastrique balances the richness of the duck. SERVES 4

4 boneless, skin-on, duck breasts

Sea salt and freshly ground pepper

½ cup chicken stock, divided

1 teaspoon arrowroot or corn starch

1 large shallot, minced (about ⅓ cup)

1 cup **Cherry-Infused Balsamic Gastrique**

1 tablespoon cold butter

Pull the skin about three-quarters of the way off each breast. Season between the meat and the skin with salt and pepper. Replace the skin and season the skin itself and the underside of the breast with salt and pepper as well. Lightly score the skin of each duck breast with a crosshatch pattern. Set aside at room temperature for 15 minutes.

Measure 2 tablespoons of chicken stock into a small bowl. Add arrowroot powder and whisk until a smooth slurry is formed. Set aside.

Preheat a large, heavy skillet over medium-high heat. Add the duck breasts to the pan, skin side down, and sear until the skin is golden brown and the fat has begun to render, about 5 minutes. Turn the breasts over and continue to cook the meat for about 3 to 5 minutes. Duck is typically served medium-rare, so the internal temperature should reach 130° F.

Remove the breasts from the pan and loosely tent with foil.

Pour off all but about 1 teaspoon of fat from the pan. (Collect the duck fat in a small jar and save it to sauté potatoes. You can thank me later!) Add the shallots, and sauté for 30 seconds. Deglaze the pan with the remaining chicken stock, using a wooden spoon to gently loosen any bits of meat and shallot from the bottom. When the chicken stock has almost simmered away, add the Cherry-Infused Balsamic Gastrique and return to a simmer. Whisk in the arrowroot slurry and simmer until the sauce has thickened slightly. Whisk in the butter and any juices that have accumulated under the resting duck breasts to make the sauce. Season to taste with salt and pepper.

Slice the duck breast thinly, crosswise, and fan across the plate or platter. Spoon the Cherry-Infused Balsamic Gastrique over the duck breasts and serve immediately.

Lemon Verbena–Infused Gastrique

Lemon Verbena–Infused Gastrique has strong, lemony flavor with light hints of licorice and camphor. I love it with chicken or fish, but especially with apricots, as you'll see in the next recipe. MAKES ABOUT ⅓ CUP

1 cup good-quality champagne vinegar or sparkling wine vinegar

1 teaspoon dried lemon verbena or 2 teaspoons chopped fresh lemon verbena

½ cup granulated sugar

2 tablespoons water

Pinch sea salt

Place the vinegar and lemon verbena in a small, nonreactive saucepan. Warm it gently over medium-low heat for 10 minutes. Cover, remove from the heat, and infuse for at least 15 minutes and as long as 1 hour. Strain out the lemon verbena and set aside.

Place the sugar and water in a medium-heavy saucepan over medium-high heat. Cook until the sugar melts and caramelizes. *Do not stir.* You can swirl the pan from time to time. Just be patient; I promise it will melt.

When the sugar has turned into liquid amber, add the infused vinegar. Again, resist the urge to stir! Swirl the pan from time to time and continue to cook until the mixture reduces and becomes syrupy, about 10 minutes.

Stir in salt and drizzle over roasted chicken or fish. You can also use this like a shrub syrup and combine it with club soda—about 2 tablespoons of syrup to 8 ounces of soda.

Unused Lemon Verbena-Infused Gastrique can be stored in the refrigerator for up to 2 weeks.

Broiled Apricots with Lemon Verbena–Infused Gastrique

This simple summer dessert is elegant and bursting with flavor. SERVES 4

6 ripe apricots

1 tablespoon caster sugar (see page 41)

2 tablespoons chopped roasted almonds

¼ cup mascarpone cheese

Lemon Verbena–Infused Gastrique

Preheat the broiler.

Wash the apricots and pat them dry. Split each apricot in half and remove the pit.

Place the apricots on a sheet pan or broiler pan, cut side up. Sprinkle each half with ¼ teaspoon of sugar.

Place the pan under the broiler. Cook the apricots until they just begin to brown, about 3 to 4 minutes.

Remove the pan from the heat and allow the apricots to cool slightly.

Place 3 apricot halves onto each of 4 dessert plates. Top each half with a heaping teaspoon of mascarpone cheese. Drizzle with Lemon Verbena–Infused Gastrique, sprinkle with toasted almonds, and serve.

Broths

7

I LOVE TO USE INFUSED BROTHS. They are some of the most versatile infusions. I think of broths as ingredients like milk or eggs versus stand-alone soups (though you can certainly enjoy them that way too). I use broths as soup bases, for sauces, in salad dressings, to flavor rice and other grains, and to poach poultry and seafood.

Most of these recipes are geared toward pre-pared broths for simplicity's sake, though the recipes can certainly be made with homemade stock for even more flavor and health benefits. The idea is that you take something common, ordinary, mundane, and give it a flavor boost. Make it sing.

The broths freeze well and can be stored up to 3 months, so I always keep a few varieties on hand. The recipes are easy to scale up. Some-times I make batches as large as a gallon—about 4 times most of the recipes. Years ago, I read that Thomas Keller, of French Laundry fame, stores his broths and stocks in freezer bags to conserve space. The bags store flat, so you can stack them. Brilliant for those of us with tiny freezers! When I need some broth, I just grab a bag, peel away the plastic, and drop the frozen broth into a pot to melt.

Shrimp & Vegetables in
Shiso-Infused Broth **Pg 139**

Ginger-Scallion-Infused Broth

You can use this broth in stir-fry recipes in place of plain chicken broth, or make your own Egg Flower Soup (see recipe). MAKES 4 CUPS

1 tablespoon safflower oil or peanut oil

½ cup sliced green onion

1 tablespoon peeled and sliced fresh ginger

4 cloves garlic, peeled and chopped

4 cups chicken broth or stock

1 tablespoon soy sauce

Pinch white pepper

Heat the oil in a large saucepan over medium heat. Add the diced green onion and ginger and sauté until the onions are soft and wilted, about 2 minutes. Stir in the garlic and cook until fragrant, about 1 minute. Pour in the chicken broth and add the remaining ingredients.

Simmer gently for 30 minutes. Strain and use or store in the refrigerator for up to 1 week.

FOR THIS INFUSION, ERIN SUGGESTS MAKING

Egg Flower Soup

My family used to go to a place called Ruby's in Madison, Wisconsin, when I was a little girl. Egg flower soup was one of my first "exotic" dining experiences. Here's my homage to Ruby. SERVES 4 TO 6

2 tablespoons arrowroot powder or cornstarch

2 tablespoons cool water

4 cups **Ginger-Scallion-Infused Broth**

Dash toasted sesame oil

2 eggs

Sea salt and white pepper, to taste

1 green onion, thinly sliced

Measure arrowroot powder into a small bowl. Add water, and whisk with a fork until the arrowroot has blended and a thin paste has formed. Set aside.

Place the Ginger-Scallion-Infused Broth in a medium saucepan. Add the sesame oil. Bring the broth to a boil over medium-high heat.

Whisk in the arrowroot paste, continuing until it is well blended. Return to a simmer and cook until slightly thickened, about 2 minutes. Reduce heat to medium.

Lightly beat the eggs in a small bowl, and season with a pinch of salt.

Stir the broth so that it creates a small vortex. Slowly stream the eggs into the swirling broth. Turn off the heat. Add white pepper and taste for additional salt. Ladle into 4 bowls or 6 cups, sprinkle with sliced green onions, and serve immediately.

Erin's Tip: You can use arrowroot powder or cornstarch in this recipe, but I like the texture of arrowroot; it blends quickly into the soup and doesn't cloud the broth.

Shiso-Infused Broth

I fell in love with shiso leaves when I was living in Japan. You often find them served with sashimi or chopped and mixed into *nato* (fermented soybeans). Their lively flavor pairs beautifully with seafood—particularly shrimp and crab. MAKES 4 CUPS

4 cups chicken stock

2 tablespoons tamari or regular soy sauce

💧 1 tablespoon **Lemongrass-Infused Rice Vinegar** (page 122)

1 tablespoon mirin

1 teaspoon honey

1 small clove garlic, thinly sliced

½ teaspoon ground ginger

2 tablespoons thinly sliced shiso leaves

Combine stock, tamari, Lemongrass-Infused Rice Vinegar, mirin, honey, garlic, and ginger in a nonreactive, medium saucepan. Whisk to combine.

Warm over medium heat until the broth begins to simmer.

When the broth is simmering, remove it from the heat and stir in the shiso leaves. Cover and allow to infuse for 5 minutes.

Shrimp & Vegetables in Shiso-Infused Broth

I love to use a Japanese mandoline to shred the daikon into noodle-like ribbons. If you prefer, you can omit the daikon and add cooked rice vermicelli noodles or bean thread noodles in their place. SERVES 4

4 cups **Shiso-Infused Broth (page 138)**

2 teaspoons toasted sesame oil

1 cup shiitake mushrooms, cleaned, stemmed, and thinly sliced

1 small carrot, peeled and thinly sliced

½ cup sliced green onion, divided

2 cups peeled and shredded daikon radish

1 cup snow peas

½ pound medium shrimp (41/50 count), peeled and deveined

2 teaspoons toasted sesame seeds

4 shiso leaves, thinly sliced chiffonade style

Sriracha sauce, for serving

In a medium saucepan, bring the Shiso-Infused Broth and sesame oil to a boil and add the shiitake mushrooms, carrot, and 6 tablespoons of green onion. Add the daikon and snow peas. Cover, reduce the heat, and simmer for 2 minutes. Add the shrimp and cook until the shrimp are just pink, 1 additional minute.

Uncover the saucepan and remove the shrimp with a slotted spoon.

Divide the broth and vegetables evenly among 4 bowls. Place the shrimp on top of each bowl of broth and vegetables. Sprinkle with the remaining 2 tablespoons of green onion, sesame seeds, and thinly sliced shiso leaves.

Serve with sriracha sauce for those who like a little spice!

What is Chiffonade?

Chiffonade is the French word for "rags." It's also a decorative cut used for broadleaf herbs like basil and mint. Chiffonade is achieved by stacking and rolling the leaves like a cigar, and then thinly slicing the cigar shape into ribbons. The effect is gossamer and elegant—a delicate garnish.

Start by washing and thoroughly drying the basil leaves. Stack the leaves, one on top of the other, with the stems and pointed tips lined up.

Starting at one long edge, roll the leaves into a tight cigar shape.

Hold the leaves snugly on the cutting board with one hand. Beginning at the tip, slice the leaves crosswise as thinly as you can.

This is one time when a very sharp knife is essential. Dull knives may not cut fully through the stack and will bruise the leaves. The outcome will be dense versus fluffy.

Citrus-Infused Chicken Broth

This broth has a Moroccan flair, so I use it to make couscous. It's also nice for making seasoned rice or braising chicken. MAKES 4 CUPS

4 cups chicken broth or stock

1 cup freshly squeezed orange juice

3 tablespoons dark brown sugar or honey

¼ teaspoon dried thyme

2 tablespoons fresh parsley, or 1 tablespoon dried

1 cinnamon stick

Pinch crushed red pepper flakes, optional

Sea salt and pepper, to taste

Combine the chicken broth, orange juice, brown sugar, thyme, parsley, and cinnamon in a medium saucepan and stir to dissolve.

Place the saucepan over medium heat. Bring to a boil, stirring occasionally. Reduce heat, and simmer for 30 minutes.

Remove from heat, cover, and continue to steep for 30 minutes. Remove the cinnamon stick and strain the finished broth.

Add the crushed red pepper flakes if using. Season with salt and pepper.

FOR THIS INFUSION, ERIN SUGGESTS MAKING

Citrus Couscous

Couscous is tiny granular pasta originally from North Africa. Cooked couscous should be light, fluffy, and lump-free. What's the key to lump-free couscous, you ask? It's simple. No stirring. It might feel counterintuitive, but resist the urge! I promise everything will turn out fine.
SERVES 4 TO 6

1½ cups uncooked couscous

2 tablespoons extra-virgin olive oil

⅓ cup sliced green onions

2¼ cups **Citrus-Infused Chicken Broth**

2 teaspoons finely grated orange zest

1 teaspoon finely grated lime zest

¼ cup chopped fresh cilantro

Sea salt, to taste

Increase heat to high and bring the broth to a boil. Remove the pan from the heat and stir in the orange zest and lime zest.

Pour the hot seasoned broth evenly over the couscous. *Do not stir.* Cover the baking dish with plastic wrap to seal. Let rest for 10 to 15 minutes, or even longer if the liquid is not all absorbed.

Rake with a fork to break up lumps. Stir in the cilantro, season with salt, and serve right away.

Erin's Tip: Purchase traditional couscous for this recipe, not the larger, pearl-size Israeli couscous.

Pour the uncooked couscous into a 9 x 13-inch baking dish.

Warm the olive oil in a medium saucepan over medium heat. Stir in the green onions and cook until slightly wilted, about 3 minutes. Pour in the Citrus-Infused Chicken Broth.

Broth aux Fines Herbes

This broth is very versatile. You can use it as the base for a fresh summer vegetable soup, pour it over dried bread for stuffing, or use it to make rice. I especially love the infusion of fresh herbs with mussels (see recipe on page 143).

MAKES 4 ½ CUPS

1 small leek

2 tablespoons butter

4 cups fish or chicken stock or broth

1 bay leaf

¼ cup chopped fresh parsley

¼ cup chopped fresh chives

2 tablespoons chopped fresh tarragon

¼ cup chopped fresh chervil or 2 tablespoons chopped fresh basil

1 sprig thyme

Cut off the root end and thick, dark green leaves of the leek. Slice the leek in half lengthwise. Rinse each half under cold running water, fanning the leaves slightly with your thumb so that the water gets in between the layers to flush out any grit. Pat the leek dry and slice thinly, crosswise.

Melt the butter in a medium saucepan over medium heat. Add the leek and cook gently until it softens and wilts, about 5 to 8 minutes.

Add the stock and the bay leaf. Increase the heat to medium-high. When stock just begins to simmer, remove it from the heat and stir in the fresh herbs. Cover the pot and allow the herbs to infuse for 5 minutes.

Remove the bay leaf and sprig of thyme before serving.

Erin's Tip: *Fines herbes* (pronounced *feenz erb*) is a classic French seasoning blend often used in omelets, over steamed potatoes, and in vinaigrettes. They typically include finely chopped parsley, chives, tarragon, and chervil, though sometimes marjoram is added.

Mussels in Broth aux Fines Herbs

The herbaceous yet delicate broth adds so much to this French classic. Try to select large, meaty mussels such as Green Lip variety. SERVES 4

3½ to 4 pounds mussels

3 tablespoons butter

1 large onion, thinly sliced

1 bay leaf

2 medium garlic cloves, sliced

1 cup **Broth aux Fines Herbs**

½ cup dry white wine or dry sherry

2 tablespoons **Fennel-Infused White Wine Vinegar** (page 123)

¼ cup heavy cream

½ teaspoon sea salt, or to taste

Freshly ground black pepper, to taste

Good-quality French bread, for serving

Place the mussels in a large bowl of cold water. Allow them to filter for at least 20 minutes, but no longer than 1 hour. Pour off the soaking water and rinse the mussels under cold water. While you are rinsing, scrub the mussels with a firm-bristled brush (or the edge of another mussel) to scrape away any debris stuck to their shells. Remove the beards (the fiberous threads that hang from the mussel shell) by pulling them toward the hinge (pointed end) of the shell. Throw out any mussels that are broken or don't close when tapped against the edge of the bowl. Place the cleaned mussels in a bowl or colander.

Melt the butter in a large, lidded pot over medium heat. Add the onion and the bay leaf. Cook until the onion slices are soft and translucent, about 10 minutes. Add the garlic and cook for another minute or so.

Add the mussels, increase the heat to high, and cover the pan. After 2 minutes, remove the lid and pour in the Broth aux Fines Herbes, wine, and Fennel-Infused White Wine Vinegar. Stir the mussels well with a large spoon. Cover the pot again and cook until the mussels have opened wide, another 3 to 4 minutes.

Remove the pot from the heat and stir in the heavy cream. Remove the bay leaf. Season with salt and pepper.

Divide the mussels among 4 shallow soup bowls. Pour the broth evenly among the bowls. Serve with bread to mop up the sauce.

Tomato-Basil-Infused Broth

Late summer is the perfect time to make this broth. The tomatoes are ripe and bursting with flavor. Use it in Fresh Garden Gazpacho (see recipe), in vinaigrette, or to poach shrimp and fish. MAKES ABOUT 1½ CUPS

2 tablespoons extra-virgin olive oil

¼ cup finely diced onion

2 small cloves garlic, thinly sliced

1½ cups Roma tomatoes (about 6 large), cored and cut into small dice

3 tablespoons chopped fresh basil leaves, or 1½ teaspoons dried

¼ teaspoon sea salt

6 whole black peppercorns

2 cups water

Splash balsamic vinegar or lemon juice

Sea salt and freshly ground black pepper, to taste

Heat the olive oil over medium heat in a medium saucepan. Add the onion and cook, stirring occasionally, until the onions have softened but not browned, about 5 to 7 minutes. Add the garlic and continue to cook until the garlic is fragrant, about 1 minute. Add the tomatoes, basil, salt, and peppercorns. Cook the tomato mixture for about 15 minutes, until it becomes softened and paste-like.

Add the water, increase the heat to high, and bring to a boil. Then reduce the heat and simmer, uncovered, for 45 minutes. Strain through a food mill or fine-mesh strainer, discarding the solids. Finish with a tiny splash of vinegar, and season with sea salt and pepper.

Use immediately or store in the refrigerator for up to 5 days.

Erin's Tip: I use a food mill to strain the broth. It removes seed and skin, so it's a time saver. If you don't have a food mill, you may wish to blanch, peel, and seed the tomatoes before you cook them down. It will make the straining easier.

Fresh Garden Gazpacho

I use Roma or other plum tomatoes for my gazpacho because they are meatier and allow me to control the thickness of the finished soup. SERVES 4 TO 6

1½ pounds Roma tomatoes (about 6 large), seeded and diced

2 cloves garlic, pressed or minced

1 medium cucumber, peeled, seeded, and diced

1 medium green, orange, or yellow bell pepper, seeded and diced

1½ teaspoons sea salt, plus more to taste

½ cup diced sweet onion, such as Walla Walla or Vidalia

1½ cups **Tomato-Basil-Infused Broth**

½ teaspoon granulated sugar, optional

2 tablespoons red wine vinegar or **Fennel-Infused White Wine Vinegar** (page 123)

¼ cup torn fresh basil leaves, divided

Freshly ground black pepper, to taste

3 to 4 tablespoons **Lemon-Infused Olive Oil** (page 98) or extra-virgin olive oil, for garnish

Place the tomatoes, garlic, cucumber, and bell pepper in a large, nonreactive bowl. Stir in 1½ teaspoons of sea salt.

Place the diced onion in a fine-mesh colander and rinse under cold running water for 1 to 2 minutes. (This helps to take the "bite" out of raw onion. You are left with pleasant onion flavor that isn't too hot or overpowering.) Drain the onions well and add to the tomato mixture.

Stir in the Tomato-Basil-Infused Broth and the sugar, if using. Place the bowl in the refrigerator and chill until completely cold, about 3 hours.

Remove the bowl from the refrigerator and stir in the vinegar and half the basil leaves. Taste for additional salt, and adjust the black pepper, if desired. Divide among soup bowls. Garnish with a drizzle of the Lemon-Infused Olive Oil and the remaining fresh basil.

Erin's Tip: Cold dulls our taste buds, so you may have to add more salt and pepper than you would expect.

Cilantro-Lime-Infused Chicken Broth

Cilantro is one of the most polarizing herbs. You either love it or you hate it. *I love it!* MAKES 4 CUPS

1 tablespoon extra-virgin olive oil

1 cup diced white onion

3 cloves garlic, chopped

4 cups chicken broth

1 bunch fresh cilantro, rinsed and patted dry

2 to 4 tablespoons freshly squeezed lime juice, to taste

Warm the olive oil in a medium saucepan over medium heat. Add the diced onions and cook until they are soft and translucent, about 10 to 12 minutes. Add the chopped garlic and cook for 1 minute longer.

Add the chicken broth. Increase heat to medium-high and bring the broth to a simmer.

While the broth is coming to a simmer, gather the clean cilantro and tie the bunch with a length of kitchen string. Hold the bundle upside-down over a cutting board (leaves toward the board/stems in the air). Use a sharp chef knife to skim the leaves away from the bundle.

Chop the leaves coarsely and set aside.

When most of the leaves have been cut away from the stems, place the tied stems into the simmering broth. Cover the pan and turn off the heat. Infuse the broth for 30 minutes.

Remove the lid and remove the cilantro stem bundle using tongs or a slotted spoon. If desired, you can strain out the onions as well.

Stir in the lime juice. Sprinkle in a handful of cilantro leaves, if desired.

Serve as a simple broth, or use the broth to make Mexican Chicken Soup (see recipe).

Erin's Tip: I really enjoy the bright citrus in this broth, especially when I use it for the Mexican Chicken Soup. If you are planning to eat the broth on its own, however, or you're using it in another recipe, you may want to reduce the amount of lime juice.

Mexican Chicken Soup (*Caldo de Pollo*)

When I lived in Northern California, we used to go to a little dive that made *the best* caldo de pollo. The memories of that soup inspired this recipe. SERVES 4 TO 6

- 2 to 3 bone-in, skin-on chicken thighs
- 4 cups **Cilantro-Lime-Infused Chicken Broth**, strained
- 1 tablespoon extra-virgin olive oil or lard
- 1 small white onion, diced
- 1 medium carrot, peeled and thinly sliced
- 1 celery stalk, sliced
- 1 medium tomato, diced
- 1 teaspoon ground cumin
- Sea salt, to taste
- ¼ cup chopped cilantro
- 1 avocado, peeled and diced, for garnish
- 1 lime, cut into wedges, for garnish
- 1 serrano chili, thinly sliced, for garnish
- White onion, diced and rinsed, for garnish

Place chicken thighs in a medium saucepan. Add the Cilantro-Lime-Infused Chicken Broth and bring to a simmer. Cover the pot and reduce the heat. Simmer until the chicken thighs are fully cooked, about 25 minutes.

In the meantime, heat the oil in a medium skillet over medium heat. Add the onion and carrot, and cook until the onions are translucent and soft, about 10 to 12 minutes. Add the celery and cook for an additional 5 minutes, until the carrots begin to soften.

Remove the chicken from the broth and set it aside to cool. Add the cooked vegetables, tomato, and cumin to the broth. Cover the saucepan and continue to cook while the chicken is cooling.

When the chicken is cool enough to handle, remove the skin and shred the meat with your fingers or a fork. Discard skin and bones. Add the shredded chicken to the broth. Salt to taste. Ladle the soup into bowls. Sprinkle each bowl with fresh cilantro. Serve the soup with bowls of optional garnish, including avocado, lime wedges, serrano chilies, and white onion, and let your guests select what garnish they'd like to add to their soup.

Caramelized-Onion Broth

This rich broth can be made with beef or chicken broth. It just depends on what you'd like to use it for. If you plan to use it for rice or stuffing, chicken broth is best. For Braised Short Ribs, French onion soup, or hearty stews, use beef broth instead (see recipe). MAKES ABOUT 6 CUPS

2 tablespoons butter

1 jumbo onion, peeled and sliced

2 large shallots, peeled and sliced

1 bay leaf

Pinch dried thyme

1 clove garlic, thinly sliced

¼ cup dry sherry or wine

4 cups beef broth or chicken broth

Sea salt and freshly ground black pepper, to taste

Melt the butter over medium heat in a large, covered skillet. When the butter has melted, stir in the onion and shallots. Cook until the onions begin to wilt slightly, about 5 to 7 minutes. Add the bay leaf and thyme, and stir to combine.

Reduce the heat to medium-low and continue to cook, stirring occasionally, until the onions are soft and caramelized, about 1 hour.

When the onions are caramelized, stir in the garlic. Cook until fragrant, about 1 to 2 minutes.

Increase the heat to medium-high. When the pan starts to sizzle, add the sherry. Deglaze the pan by stirring and scraping the bottom with a wooden spoon while the sherry cooks away. When the sherry has evaporated, stir in the broth. Bring the broth to a simmer. Cover the pan, turn off the heat, and allow the broth to infuse for 1 hour.

When the broth is infused, you can strain out the onions if you wish. Remove the bay leaf and season the broth with salt and pepper. Store any unused broth in the refrigerator for up to 1 week.

Braised Short Ribs

There is nothing like the rich flavor of slow-braised beef! SERVES 4 TO 6

4 pounds bone-in beef short ribs, cut into 2-inch pieces

Sea salt and freshly ground black pepper, to taste

1 teaspoon dried thyme

2 to 3 tablespoons clarified butter

2 cups thickly sliced carrots

4 whole garlic cloves, peeled and slightly crushed

1 tablespoon tomato paste

½ cup red wine

2 tablespoons potato starch or cornstarch

3 cups **Caramelized-Onion Broth,** divided

1 bay leaf

1 teaspoon dried rosemary

2 teaspoons red wine vinegar

Season the short ribs with salt, pepper, and thyme. Cover and refrigerate until 1 hour before cooking.

Preheat the oven to 325°F.

Heat butter in a Dutch oven or oven-safe pot with a snug-fitting lid over medium-high heat. Brown the short ribs on all sides, turning every 3 to 5 minutes. Remove short ribs to a plate, and loosely tent with aluminum foil.

Add the carrots and cook, stirring occasionally, until they begin to brown, about 5 minutes. Add the garlic cloves and tomato paste, and cook until fragrant, 1 to 2 minutes.

Add the red wine, and deglaze the pan, scraping the bottom of the pot gently with a wooden spoon to loosen any browned bits of meat and vegetables.

Place the potato starch in a small bowl. Measure ½ cup of the Caramelized-Onion Broth and strain; reserve the onions. Slowly combine the broth with the potato starch, whisking until you have a smooth slurry. Pour the slurry, the strained onions, and the remaining 2½ cups broth into the vegetables. Add the bay leaf and rosemary and stir to blend.

Add the ribs, bone side up. Pour any juices that accumulated on the plate into the pot. Cover tightly with a lid and place in the oven. Simmer, covered, 2½ to 3½ hours, until meat is tender and starts falling off the bone.

Lift the ribs out of the braising liquid and set aside on a warm platter. Tent with aluminum foil.

Place the braising liquid in the refrigerator to cool for 20 to 30 minutes. The fat will harden and form a layer on the top of the liquid as it cools. Use a spoon to lift away as much of the fat as you can, and discard. Return the Dutch oven to the stove top. Cook over high heat until the liquid boils. Cook, stirring, until the mixture reduces by about one-fourth. Remove the bay leaf, stir in the red wine vinegar, and return the short ribs to the pot. (You can add the whole ribs or simply pull the meat from the bones and return it to the pot.) Warm through. Spoon the ribs and braising liquid over mashed potatoes or creamy polenta.

Desserts

8

DESSERTS OFFER UNIQUE OPPORTUNITIES for infusions—from infused honeys and sugars to fabulous creamy concoctions. I offer a variety of desserts, most of which start out with a liquid base.

One of the most fun aspects of this chapter was including some unexpected ingredients. My greatest inspiration came from Karen Page and Andrew Dornenburg's book *The Flavor Bible*. It emboldened me to experiment with new and unique flavor combinations. If you are looking for more ways to stretch your culinary creativity, their book is a must.

Savory herbs feature prominently in several recipes, and I love the results. The subtle piney, caramel sweetness dripping off fresh peaches is divine. The light licorice freshness of whipped cream over ripe melon is mouthwatering. The basil-lime semifreddo is a fragrant counterpoint to the tang of strawberry sorbet. It's easy to wax romantic about these desserts.

This chapter is purely decadent and was an absolute pleasure to write, test, taste, test, taste, test, and taste. You get the idea. I may have put on a couple of pounds in the name of perfection. All worth it!

Basil-Lime-Infused Semifreddo
with Strawberry Sorbet **Pg 164**

Lavender-Lemon-Infused Syrup for Sorbet

Adding a little bit of vodka to this sorbet syrup keeps it from freezing solid, so it's just soft enough to scoop. MAKES 1 QUART

- 2 cups filtered water
- 2 cups granulated sugar
- 2 tablespoons dried culinary lavender
- 1 tablespoon finely grated lemon zest
- 2 cups freshly squeezed lemon juice, strained
- 2 tablespoons vodka, optional

Pour the water into a medium saucepan. Add the sugar and stir to blend. Cook over medium-high heat until the sugar has dissolved and the water is simmering, about 5 to 7 minutes.

Remove the pan from the heat and stir in the lavender and lemon zest. Cover the pan and allow to infuse for 20 minutes.

Strain the Lavender-Lemon-Infused Syrup through a fine-mesh strainer into a bowl. Stir in the lemon juice and vodka.

Place the bowl in the refrigerator to cool. Chill until completely cold.

FOR THIS INFUSION, ERIN SUGGESTS MAKING

Lavender-Lemon-Infused Sorbet

Pour the cold Lavender-Lemon-Infused Syrup into an ice cream maker and process according to manufacturer's directions. When the sorbet is set, serve or transfer to a covered container, and freeze for up to 1 month.

To serve, spoon into pretty bowls and sprinkle with fresh organic lavender flowers, if desired.

Ginger-Infused Honey

Ginger-infused honey is great for sore throats *or* gelato! MAKES 1 CUP

1 cup honey

**Scant ¼ cup peeled and minced ginger
(about a 3-inch piece)**

Scrape the honey into a small saucepan. Heat gently over low heat. It's important not to overheat the honey. If you are using raw honey, you should not heat it over 118° F. Use a candy thermometer to control the temperature. A double boiler is an even gentler way to warm the honey.

Stir in the ginger and continue to heat for 10 minutes. Remove the pan from the heat and cover. Let the honey steep for 15 minutes. Stir once or twice while steeping.

Pour the still-warm honey through a fine-mesh strainer to remove the ginger.

Store the honey in a sterile jar with a tight-fitting lid in a dark cupboard for up to 6 months.

Ginger-Infused-Honey Gelato with Crème Fraîche

I used crème fraîche in this recipe to balance the ginger and honey. It's a bit more elegant and unusual. If you can't find crème fraîche in your local grocery store, it's easy to make. There's a recipe for it in my book, *The Kitchen Pantry Cookbook*.

SERVES 6 TO 8

- 2 cups whole milk
- 1 cup heavy cream
- ¾ cup **Ginger-Infused Honey**
- 6 large egg yolks
- 1¾ cup crème fraîche
- ¼ cup (1.5 ounces) chopped candied ginger, plus additional for garnish

Place the milk and heavy cream in a medium saucepan over medium-low heat. Cook, whisking occasionally, until the milk mixture reaches about 170°F, about 15 to 20 minutes.

Beat the egg yolks until blended. Add the Ginger-Infused Honey and whisk until smooth, thick, and pale amber in color.

Ladle ½ cup of the milk mixture into the yolks, and whisk well. Add an additional ½ cup of the warm milk mixture, and whisk until well blended.

Pour the warmed egg mixture back into the saucepan. Cook over medium heat, stirring constantly, until the mixture thickens and can coat the back of a spoon, about 20 minutes. Do not boil.

Pour the custard through a strainer into a medium bowl. Press a layer of plastic wrap or wax paper against the surface to prevent a skin from forming. Place the bowl in the refrigerator, and chill thoroughly for several hours.

Stir the crème fraîche into the chilled custard. Pour the mixture into your ice cream maker and process according to manufacturer's directions. After about 10 minutes, add the chopped candied ginger and continue to process.

When the gelato is set, transfer it to a lidded glass or plastic container. Lay a piece of wax paper over the gelato and close the lid. Freeze overnight.

When you are ready to serve, scoop the gelato into serving bowls. Garnish with additional candied ginger.

Cardamom-Infused Orange Juice for Sherbet

Orange sherbet on its own—delicious! Infusing cardamom gives it an exotic twist.

MAKES ABOUT 1 QUART

2 tablespoons green cardamom pods

2 cups freshly squeezed orange juice from about 5 or 6 large Valencia oranges

1 tablespoon finely grated orange zest

1 tablespoon freshly squeezed lemon juice

¾ cup granulated sugar

⅛ teaspoon sea salt

1½ cups half-and-half or whole milk

Chopped toasted pistachios for garnish, optional

Crush the cardamom pods using a mortar and pestle. If you don't have a mortar and pestle, you can put the pods in a plastic bag with a zipper closure and crush them with a heavy pan or rolling pin.

Place the crushed cardamom pods and seeds, orange juice, orange zest, lemon juice, sugar, and salt into a medium saucepan. Cook over medium heat until the sugar dissolves. Cover and remove from the heat. Allow the juice to infuse for 20 minutes.

Strain the infused juice through a fine-mesh strainer into a medium nonreactive bowl. Discard the zest, pulp, and cardamom pods. Refrigerate until completely chilled, about 2 hours.

Stir in the half-and-half and pour the blended mixture into an ice cream maker. Process according to manufacturer's directions.

Transfer the sherbet to a covered container and freeze until firm, at least 3 hours or as long as overnight. Serve sprinkled with toasted pistachios, if desired.

Unused sherbet can be stored in the freezer, tightly covered, for up to 1 month.

What *is* Cardamom?

Cardamom pods are the seedpods of various ginger plants. The two main types are black cardamom and green cardamom. Both are common in Indian cooking, turning up in everything from curries to basmati rice to chai (see page 35). The green is much more aromatic—at once both citrusy and musty-minty. Smoky-sweet black cardamom is a key ingredient in garam masala, a famous Indian spice blend.

You can buy whole pods or ground seeds. I chose the green pods for the sherbet because the citrus undertones pair well with orange. I use ground green cardamom on glazed carrots, in carrot soup, and rhubarb chutney or compote. Black cardamom can enhance lentil and rice dishes.

Lemon-Infused Honey

This honey is so fragrant and bright. Add it to green tea or simply stir it into in a mug of hot water for a comforting treat.

½ cup honey

1 tablespoon finely grated lemon zest

Place the honey and lemon zest in a medium saucepan. Warm gently over medium-low heat for about 15 minutes. If you have a candy thermometer, you can use it to monitor the temperature. It should hover around 115° F. Remove the warm honey from the stovetop, cover, and infuse for 1 hour.

FOR THIS INFUSION, ERIN SUGGESTS MAKING

Lemon-Infused-Honey Mousse

Try layering this light, creamy mousse with berries and granola for a gorgeous parfait.

SERVES 4

💧 **½ cup Lemon-Infused Honey**

½ cup freshly squeezed lemon juice

½ cup (1 stick) chilled butter, cut into pieces, divided

4 large egg yolks

1 large egg

½ cup chilled heavy cream

Grated lemon zest and fresh berries for garnish, optional

Combine the Lemon-Infused Honey, lemon juice, and ¼ cup of the butter in a medium saucepan. Cook over medium heat, whisking constantly, until the butter has melted and the mixture is fully blended. Remove from heat.

Whisk egg yolks and egg in the top of a double boiler or heatproof medium bowl. Set the double boiler (or bowl) over a saucepan of gently simmering water and cook, stirring constantly, until the mixture is pale and thick, about 2 minutes.

Slowly pour the warm lemon mixture into the egg mixture, whisking constantly. Place the bowl over the simmering water, reduce the heat to medium-low, and cook, whisking constantly, until the curd is thickened and the whisk leaves a trail, about 5 minutes. Remove from the heat and add the remaining ¼ cup butter, whisking until melted and the curd is smooth.

Strain the curd through a fine-mesh strainer into a bowl. Cover with plastic wrap, pressing directly onto the surface. This ensures that a skin won't form on the curd while it's cooling. Refrigerate until completely chilled, at least 2 hours.

Just before serving, whisk the cream in a bowl until stiff peaks form. Then gently fold the whipped cream into the curd, scooping from the outside of the bowl toward the center so the cream doesn't deflate too much. When the mousse is thoroughly blended, spoon into serving dishes. Top with a few fresh berries and lemon zest, if desired.

Rosemary-Infused Brown Sugar

In general, dried herbs and flowers are best for infusing sugar. The moisture in fresh herbs can cause clumping. Since brown sugar is moist to begin with, however, adding fresh herbs is just fine. MAKES 1 CUP

4 to 5 four-inch sprigs fresh rosemary

1 cup light brown sugar

Wash and thoroughly dry the rosemary sprigs. If you have time, lay them on a clean kitchen towel to dry overnight.

Rub the leaves of the sprigs between your fingers to release their fragrance. Place them in a sterile jar with a tight-fitting lid. Be sure the jar is large enough to leave some room on top of the sugar—an inch is ideal.

Add the brown sugar and close the jar. Shake vigorously to blend the herbs into the sugar.

Shake the jar every day or two. Allow to infuse for at least 1 week. Remove the sprigs before using. Store the sugar in a cool, dry place for up to 3 weeks.

Erin's Tip: Rosemary sugar makes a great rub for pork tenderloin or baby back ribs. It's also lovely on roasted squash.

Roasted Peaches with Rosemary-Infused Brown Sugar

You can substitute plums or fresh figs for the peaches too! SERVES 4 TO 8

4 ripe peaches, freestone if you can find them

4 teaspoons butter, plus extra for buttering baking sheet

1 to 2 teaspoons **Rosemary-Infused Brown Sugar**

½ cup ricotta cheese

2 teaspoons honey

½ teaspoon freshly squeezed lemon juice

2 to 3 tablespoons sliced almonds, lightly toasted

Chopped fresh rosemary leaves, for garnish, optional

Preheat oven to 425°F.

Wash and pat the peaches dry. Halve them by splitting along the divot at the stem of the peach. Insert your knife into the divot at the stem end. When you feel the pit, begin to turn the peach in a circle, following the natural line, until you end up at the initial cut. Take the peach in both hands and gently twist each half in opposite directions to separate the two halves. Use a paring knife to remove the pit. Repeat with remaining peaches.

Place the peaches, cut side down, on a buttered, rimmed baking sheet.

Place the pan in the oven and roast until the peaches are just softened, about 10 minutes, depending on their ripeness.

Remove the pan from the oven. Use tongs to turn the peaches over so the cut side is facing up. Place ½ teaspoon of butter in the center of each peach. Sprinkle with the Rosemary-Infused Brown Sugar.

Return the pan to the oven and continue to roast until the sugar has melted, about 5 minutes. Remove the peaches from the oven, and allow them to cool slightly.

To caramelize the rosemary sugar, use a kitchen torch or your broiler. If broiling, place the peaches about 4 inches from the heat source for about 1 to 2 minutes. Keep a close watch to make sure the sugar doesn't burn.

While the peaches are caramelizing, place the ricotta, honey, and lemon juice in a small bowl. Stir or beat to combine.

Remove the peaches from the oven. Allow to cool slightly or to room temperature. Top with sweetened ricotta, and sprinkle with toasted almonds and chopped rosemary, if using.

Bay Leaf–Infused Cream for Ice Cream

It's fun to take an ingredient such as bay that is most often used in savory dishes and add it to a dessert! MAKES ABOUT 1 QUART

2 cups heavy cream

1 cup whole milk

8 fresh bay leaves

4 egg yolks, beaten

⅔ cup granulated sugar

⅛ teaspoon sea salt

Freshly grated nutmeg, for garnish

Pour the heavy cream and milk into a heavy medium saucepan. Add the bay leaves. Cook over medium-high heat until the cream blend reaches a simmer, about 5 minutes. Remove the cream blend from the heat, cover, and let infuse for 20 minutes. Remove the bay leaves from the cream with a slotted spoon.

Place the egg yolks, sugar, and salt into a medium bowl and whisk until fully blended and slightly frothy. Next, slowly stream in about ¼ of the Bay Leaf–Infused Cream, whisking constantly. Repeat with an additional ¼ of the cream. Slowly whisk in the remaining cream.

Return the cream blend to the saucepan. Place over medium-low heat and cook, whisking constantly, until the cream thickens to a custard.

Remove the custard from the heat. Strain the custard through a fine-mesh strainer into a clean bowl. Lay a layer of plastic wrap over the custard, pressing it to the surface. Place the bowl in the refrigerator to chill completely. This will take at least 2 hours and as long as overnight.

When the custard is fully chilled, pour it into an ice cream maker and mix according to the manufacturer's direction. When the ice cream is set, serve with a light grating of fresh nutmeg for garnish.

Tarragon-Infused Cream Topping for Ripe Melons

This cold infusion intensifies the flavor of the tarragon whipped cream. You might also enjoy it on apricots or dark sweet cherries. SERVES 4 TO 8

1 cup heavy cream

2 tablespoons caster sugar (see page 41)

2 tablespoons chopped fresh tarragon

1 ripe cantaloupe, peeled, seeded and cut into 8 to 16 wedges

Tarragon sprigs or fresh tarragon leaves, for garnish, optional

Place the cream, sugar, and chopped tarragon in a jar or glass bowl. Stir to blend.

Cover and refrigerate for 24 hours.

Stir the infusion to be sure the sugar has fully dissolved. Strain the cream into a chilled bowl and whip to stiff peaks.

Arrange wedges of melon on plates. Dollop some Tarragon-Infused Cream Topping onto the melon wedges. Garnish with a sprig of tarragon or some fresh tarragon leaves, if desired. Serve.

Herbed Simple Syrups

You can infuse simple syrups with fresh or dried herbs. Try your own combinations to create unique flavors for cocktails, soft drinks and ice teas, or sorbets! Here are some general guidelines.

For traditional simple syrup, use a ratio of 1 to 1 sugar to water. If you think you'll be using your syrup for cocktails, you may want to make rich simple syrup, which is a 2-to-1 ratio of sugar to water.

The type of sugar is up to you—granulated, caster, turbinado, demerara, even brown sugar— but granulated sugar and caster sugar are the most neutral, so they let the herbs shine. Plus, they dissolve more quickly in water. I use turbinado or demerara sugars when caramel undertones would enhance the flavor—a rum or bourbon cocktail, for example. Brown sugar can be used if a molasses flavor is what you are looking for, but remember it might overpower your herbs.

If you are using fresh herbs, wash them first. The amount of fresh herbs varies, but a big handful or a loosely packed cup is a good place to start. If an herb is particularly strong, like rosemary, try using 3 or 4 sprigs to begin with.

Fresh herbs provide the most robust flavor and aroma, but dried herbs can be used too. However, the essential oils in dried herbs may have dissipated over time. To counteract that, you may need to add a little more or infuse a little longer. Start with a couple of tablespoons, and see if you like the strength and flavor.

To make simple syrup, pour the sugar and water into a small saucepan. Bring the water to boil over medium-high to high heat. Stir until the sugar has completely dissolved.

Take the simple syrup off the heat. Stir in the herbs. Cover and let steep for 1 to 2 hours.

Strain the infused syrup through a fine-mesh sieve—or in the case of dried herbs, several layers of moistened cheesecloth—into a sterile bottle or jar. Store in the refrigerator for up to 6 months.

Lemongrass-Infused Coconut Milk for Popsicles

I like using coconut palm sugar. It's lower on the glycemic index than cane sugars and pairs tastily with the coconut milk and lemongrass.

MAKES 10 THREE-OUNCE POPSICLES

2 cans (14-ounces each) full-fat coconut milk

2 stalks lemongrass

⅓ rounded cup coconut palm sugar or granulated sugar

2 teaspoons finely grated lime zest

2 teaspoons freshly squeezed lime juice

Gently shake the cans of coconut milk to blend. Open the cans and pour them into a medium saucepan.

Cut away the roots and any green leaves of the lemongrass to leave about 6 inches of white and pale yellow-green stalk. Use a mallet or heavy pan to smash the stalks.

Place the crushed lemongrass stalks into the coconut milk. Stir in the sugar. Simmer over medium heat, stirring occasionally, until the sugar has dissolved and fully blended, about 7 to 10 minutes. Remove the pan from the heat. Cover and allow the lemongrass to infuse for 45 minutes.

Strain the Lemongrass-Infused Coconut Milk through a fine-mesh sieve into a large measuring cup or pitcher. Stir in the lime zest and juice.

Pour the coconut milk mixture into 10 Popsicle molds, dividing evenly. Cover and insert the sticks. Place the Popsicles in a freezer until fully set, about 6 hours.

When the Popsicles are fully frozen, loosen them from the molds with warm water, and serve immediately.

Basil-Lime-Infused Semifreddo with Strawberry Sorbet

See photo Pg 151. Semifreddo is a frozen mousse dessert. I decided to layer this one with sorbet.

SERVES 8 TO 12

FOR THE CUSTARD:

3 large egg yolks

1½ teaspoons finely grated lime zest

¼ cup lime juice

Pinch sea salt

¾ cup caster sugar (page 41), divided

1 tablespoon chiffonade-cut basil leaves

1 cup heavy cream

FOR THE SORBET:

1½ pounds strawberries (about 4 cups), hulled and sliced

⅔ cup granulated sugar or caster sugar

1½ teaspoons freshly squeezed lemon juice

Pinch sea salt

Whisk together the egg yolks, lime zest and juice, salt, and ½ cup of the sugar in the top of a double boiler or heatproof medium bowl. Set the double boiler (or bowl) over a saucepan of gently simmering water and cook, stirring constantly, until the mixture has thickened slightly, 12 to 15 minutes.

Place a fine-mesh sieve over a medium bowl. Pour the lime mixture through the sieve into the bowl. Stir in the chiffonade-cut basil leaves. Tuck plastic wrap onto the surface of the Basil-Lime-Infused Custard mixture and let the mixture infuse until cool, about 1 hour.

Line an 8 x 4-inch loaf pan with plastic wrap.

Using an electric mixer, whip the cream and the remaining ¼ cup of sugar on medium until soft peaks form, 2 to 3 minutes. When the cream is whipped, gently fold it into the basil-lime infusion.

Pour into the plastic lined loaf pan, cover, and freeze until firm, at least 4 hours.

While the semifreddo is setting up, make the sorbet. Place the strawberries into a blender or food processor and purée until smooth. Add the sugar and lemon juice and salt and continue to purée until the sugar is fully incorporated, about 1 minute. The liquid should equal about 3 cups.

Transfer the sorbet base to a bowl or dish and place in the refrigerator to chill, about 2 hours or until very cold.

Pour the chilled sorbet into an ice cream maker and churn according to manufacturers' recommendations, about 20 to 25 minutes.

Spread the churned sorbet over the frozen semifreddo and freeze at least 2 hours, or until the sorbet has hardened. Slice and serve on chilled plates.

Oven-Roasted Balsamic Strawberries with Mint Granita

Sweet, refreshing, and delightfully summery! SERVES 4 TO 6

- 1 cup tightly packed mint leaves, any variety you like
- ¼ teaspoon **Mint Extract** (page 44)
- ½ cup caster sugar (page 41)
- 2 cups water
- 2 tablespoons freshly squeezed lemon juice
- 1 tablespoon vodka
- 2 pints large ripe strawberries
- 1 to 2 tablespoons granulated sugar
- 2 tablespoons balsamic vinegar
- 4 to 6 mint sprigs, for garnish, optional

Place the mint leaves, Mint Extract, caster sugar, and water into a medium saucepan. Stir to combine. Bring the mixture to a simmer, stirring occasionally. When the sugar has dissolved, remove the herbed simple syrup from the heat, cover, and let steep for 10 minutes.

Stir in the lemon juice and vodka. Strain the syrup through a fine-mesh strainer. (Don't worry if a few mint flecks make it through.) Place the strained syrup in the refrigerator to chill for at least 1 hour.

Pour the chilled syrup into a lasagna pan or rectangular, nonreactive metal pan. Place the pan in the freezer. Set a timer for 30 minutes.

When the timer goes off, rake the freezing syrup with a fork to break up any large clumps. Set the timer for another 30 minutes and return the mixture to the freezer. Continue this process of freezing and raking at 30-minute intervals for 2 to 3 hours. The resulting granita will be frosty-slushy, like Hawaiian Snow.

While the granita is setting up, preheat oven to 375° F.

Wash and hull the strawberries. Pat them dry and place them in a large bowl. Sprinkle with granulated sugar. Add the balsamic vinegar and stir to combine.

Spread the strawberries onto a rimmed baking sheet. Roast until the strawberries are slightly softened but not mushy, about 10 minutes. Remove the pan from the oven, and cool to room temperature.

Divide the cooled balsamic berries among 4 to 6 bowls. Top with a small scoop of mint granita, and garnish with a sprig of mint, if desired. Serve.

Jasmine Tea–Infused Cream for Panna Cotta with Mango Purée

This is one sexy dessert! Creamy and fragrant with a pop of mango. Oh baby!

SERVES 6

3 cups half-and-half or mixture of 1½ cups heavy cream and 1½ cups whole milk

3 tablespoons loose-leaf jasmine or vanilla tea

½ cup granulated sugar

3 tablespoons cold water

2 teaspoons unflavored gelatin

1 teaspoon coconut oil or vegetable oil for custard cups/ramekins

1 ripe mango or 1 cup frozen mango chunks

1 to 2 tablespoons granulated sugar

2 teaspoons freshly squeezed lime juice

Heat half-and-half in a medium saucepan over medium-high heat until it is just simmering. Remove the pan from the stovetop and stir in the tea and sugar. Stir until the sugar has dissolved. Cover with a snug-fitting lid, and steep for 1 hour.

When the cream has steeped, it's time to "bloom" the gelatin (see Erin's Tip). Put the water in a small bowl and sprinkle in the gelatin. Allow to bloom for 5 minutes.

Strain the Jasmine Tea–Infused Cream through a fine-mesh sieve into a pitcher or bowl with a spout.

Place the small bowl containing the bloomed gelatin into a hot-water bath to melt it. Be sure the water bath is shallow so that you don't accidentally splash water into the gelatin. Alternatively, you can place the small bowl of bloomed gelatin in a microwave on high for 10 seconds to melt it. The gelatin should become liquid and translucent. You may need to stir it gently to be sure all the granules have dissolved.

Rinse the saucepan to wash away any leftover tea leaves. Return 1 cup of strained, infused cream to the pan, along with the liquefied gelatin. Place the pan over medium heat and cook, stirring constantly, until the gelatin is fully blended. Stir in the remaining infused cream.

Lightly coat six 4-ounce custard cups or ramekins with the coconut oil. Ladle the cream into the prepared cups. Refrigerate until set, about 3 hours. While the panna cotta is setting up, make the mango purée.

If using fresh mango, peel and dice the mango, discarding the center pit. Place the diced mango in a food processor, along with sugar and lime juice. Purée until smooth. Cover and chill the purée until the panna cotta is set.

When the panna cotta is set, spoon the mango purée thickly over the top, and serve.

Erin's Tip: "Blooming" means placing gelatin in liquid. The gelatin granules absorb the liquid and get larger. The result is kind of like cold Cream of Wheat cereal—a little gloppy. The next step is to melt the glop—I mean the bloomed gelatin. I suggest a hot-water bath or a quick few seconds in the microwave. The gelatin will liquefy, and then it's ready to blend into whatever you are making.

Spice-Infused Caramel Sauce with Poached Pears

Poached pears are classic. The addition of this spiced, salted caramel gives this dessert a modern twist. SERVES 6

3 firm, ripe Anjou pears, peeled, halved, and cored

3 tablespoons freshly squeezed lemon juice

1 bottle dry white wine, such as Pinot Grigio or Sauvignon Blanc

Zest and juice of 1 large lemon

1¾ cups granulated sugar, divided

1 three-inch-piece cinnamon stick

¼ cup water

1½ cups heavy cream

¼ teaspoon sea salt

1 whole clove

5 green cardamom pods

¼ teaspoon anise seeds

¼ teaspoon whole black peppercorns

Mascarpone cheese or vanilla ice cream, for serving

⅓ cup chopped toasted almonds, hazelnuts, or pistachios, for garnish, if desired

Peel, core, and halve the pears. Place the pears in a bowl and toss with lemon juice. Set aside.

Combine the wine, lemon zest and juice, 1 cup of the sugar, and the cinnamon stick in a large, covered pot. Cook over medium heat until the sugar melts and the mixture begins to simmer, about 7 minutes.

Add the pears to the simmering liquid. Cover and simmer until the pears are just tender, about 10 to 25 minutes, depending on how ripe they are. (Don't overcook the pears. They will continue to cook as they cool.) Remove the lid and allow the pears to cool in the poaching liquid.

In the meantime, combine the remaining ¾ cup sugar and water in a medium saucepan. Stir to combine. Melt the sugar over medium heat. *Do not stir* during the melting process. Continue to heat the sugar over medium heat until the water has simmered away and the sugar has become amber colored and caramelized. Carefully stir in the cream, salt, clove, cardamom pods, anise, and peppercorns.

Warning: The mixture is going to sputter and bubble at first, and the caramel will harden slightly. Just keep stirring. Simmer the caramel, stirring constantly, until the sauce is reduced to about 1 cup, about 10 minutes.

Pour the Spice-Infused Caramel Sauce through a fine-mesh sieve into a small heat-resistant bowl or measuring cup. Cover and set aside.

Drain and pat the pears dry. Place one pear half on each of six dessert plates. Place a small scoop of mascarpone cheese or vanilla ice cream in the hollow of the pear, and drizzle with Spice-Infused Caramel Sauce. Sprinkle with toasted nuts, if using. Serve immediately.

Erin's Tip: Pears can be poached and then chilled prior to serving.

Lemon Verbena–Infused Cream for Pots de Crème

This lightly herbed cream is subtle and elegant. SERVES 6

1 cup heavy cream

¾ cup milk

4 tablespoons fresh lemon verbena leaves or 2 tablespoons dried

6 large egg yolks

⅓ cup caster sugar (see page 41)

💧 ½ teaspoon **Lemon Extract** (page 41)

Fresh blueberries, raspberries, or strawberries, for garnish, optional

Preheat oven to 325°F.

Pour the heavy cream and milk into a medium saucepan. Add the lemon verbena. Cook the cream blend over medium-high heat. When it begins to simmer, cover the pan and remove from the heat. Allow to infuse for 30 minutes.

While the cream blend is infusing, whisk together the egg yolks and caster sugar until pale yellow and frothy.

Whisk the Lemon Verbena–Infused Cream into the egg and sugar mixture, a ladle at a time. When the cream and eggs are fully blended, stir in the lemon extract. Strain the custard base through a fine-mesh strainer into ½-cup ramekins. Discard the lemon verbena leaves.

Cover each ramekin with foil. Place the ramekins in a large lasagna pan, or similar shallow pan. Add boiling water to the pan so that the water comes halfway up the ramekins.

Place the pan in the oven and bake the custards until they are just set, about 45 to 55 minutes. The center of the custard should jiggle ever so slightly when you shimmy the ramekin.

Remove the custards from the water. Remove the foil and transfer the custards to the refrigerator to chill, for at least 3 hours. Once they are completely chilled, cover them with plastic wrap or foil until you are ready to eat them.

When you are ready to serve, uncover the custards, and top with fresh berries, if desired.

Erin's Tip: You can make the custards a day or two ahead of time, if you like.

Orange-Infused Olive Oil Cake

Since this cake contains no flour and is more delicate than a traditional cake, I recommend using a springform cake pan. SERVES 8 TO 12

4 large egg yolks

1 cup caster sugar, divided (see page 41)

6 tablespoons **Orange-Infused Olive Oil** (page 98)

Zest of 1 orange

Zest of 1 lemon

¼ teaspoon **Orange Extract** (page 41)

1¾ cups almond meal/almond flour

6 egg whites

Powdered sugar, for garnish

Preheat oven to 350°F.

Butter a 10-inch springform cake pan. You can add a round of buttered parchment paper to the bottom of the pan if you like. I typically serve the cake directly from the springform pan, but if you plan to move it to a cake stand, parchment paper will add stability. Set the pan aside.

Using a hand mixer or stand mixer, beat the egg yolks, ¾ cup caster sugar, and Orange-Infused Olive Oil mixture until it's light and pale yellow. Beat in the orange zest, lemon zest, and Orange Extract. Add the almond meal, and combine well.

Clean the beaters and use them to beat the egg whites into soft peaks. Add the remaining ¼ cup caster sugar, and continue to beat until stiff peaks form.

Fold the stiff egg whites gently into the almond meal batter. Mix until blended.

Pour the batter into the prepared springform pan. Bake for 30 to 35 minutes, or until the cake is golden brown and feels firm to the touch.

Place the cake pan on a cooling rack and allow to cool completely before releasing the latch. Use a butter knife to loosen the cake from the edge of the pan. Release the latch and lift off the cake ring.

Just before serving, sprinkle the top of the cake with powdered sugar. I usually use a tea strainer or small sieve for this. Serve.

Metric Conversions

Metric Volume Conversions

US Volume Measure	Metric Equivalent
⅛ teaspoon	0.5 milliliters
¼ teaspoon	1 milliliter
½ teaspoon	2.5 milliliters
¾ teaspoon	4 milliliters
1 teaspoon	5 milliliters
1¼ teaspoons	6 milliliters
1½ teaspoons	7.5 milliliters
1¾ teaspoons	8.5 milliliters
2 teaspoons	10 milliliters
½ tablespoon	7.5 milliliters
1 tablespoon (3 teaspoons, ½ fluid ounce)	15 milliliters
2 tablespoons (1 fluid ounce)	30 milliliters
¼ cup (4 tablespoons)	60 milliliters
⅓ cup	90 milliliters
½ cup (4 fluid ounces)	125 milliliters
⅔ cup	160 milliliters
¾ cup (6 fluid ounces)	180 milliliters
1 cup (16 tablespoons, 8 fluid ounces)	250 milliliters
1¼ cups	300 milliliters
1½ cups (12 fluid ounces)	360 milliliters
1⅔ cups	400 milliliters
2 cups (1 pint)	500 Milliliters
3 cups	700 Milliliters
4 cups (1 quart)	950 milliliters
1 quart plus ¼ cup	1 liter
4 quarts (1 gallon)	3.8 liters

Metric Weight Conversions

US Weight Measure	Metric Equivalent
½ ounce	7 grams
½ ounce	15 grams
¾ ounce	21 grams
1 ounce	28 grams
1¼ ounces	35 grams
1½ ounces	42.5 grams
1⅔ ounces	45 grams
2 ounces	57 grams
3 ounces	85 grams
4 ounces (¼ pound)	113 grams
5 ounces	142 grams
6 ounces	170 grams
7 ounces	198 grams
8 ounces (½ pound)	227 grams
12 ounces (¾ pound)	340 Grams
16 ounces (1 pound)	454 grams
32.5 ounces (2.2 pounds)	1 kilogram

Temperature Conversions

Degrees Fahrenheit	Degrees Celsius
200° F	100° C
250° F	120° C
275° F	140° C
300° F	150° C
325° F	160° C
350° F	180° C
375° F	190° C
400° F	200° C
425° F	220° C
450° F	230° C
475° F	246° C

Index

Resources

Beanilla
*Leading supplier of
vanilla beans, pure extracts,
natural flavorings, and
baking ingredients*
www.beanilla.com
sales@beanilla.com
888.261.3384

Chefshop.com
*Artisan, quality products
from around the world*
www.chefshop.com
800.596.0885

Felix Doolittle
*Gorgeous chef medallions,
canning labels, and oval
kitchen labels*
www.felixdoolittle.com
hello@felixdoolittle.com
617.969.8883

Glass Bottle Outlet
*Glass and plastic bottles,
jugs, and jars*
www.glassbottleoutlet.com
customerservice@
    glassbottleoutlet.com
844.230.0181
888.395.6551

Katz Farm
*Orleans' method vinegars,
organic California olive oils,
and other artisan food*
www.katzandco.com
info@katzfarm.com
800.676.7176

Mountain Rose Herbs
*Bulk herbs, spices,
and loose-leaf teas*
www.mountainroseherbs.com
800.879.3337
support@
    mountainroseherbs.com

Prodyne
Fruit infusion beverage ware
prodyne.com
info@prodyne.com
800.822.4776
Found at many top retailers

SpiceJungle
*Gourmet spices, herbs,
and hard-to-find culinary
ingredients from around
the world*
www.spicejungle.com
sales@spicejungle.com
888.261.3384

Tenzing Momo
*Apothecary herbs,
bittering agents, and
barks for root beer*
www.tenzingmomo.com
206.623.9837

Tillen Farms
*Northwest fresh!
Pickled vegetables
and preserved cherries
including Bada Bing Cherries*
www.tillenfarms.com
info@tillenfarms.com
212.957.0055
Toll-free 855.972.0516

Meet Erin Coopey

Erin Coopey is a chef, writer, cooking instructor, and professional speaker in Seattle, Washington. After receiving her culinary degree, Erin trained at the prestigious Culinary Institute of America at Greystone. She has molded her passion into a career, sharing her love of cooking and good food with hundreds of students.

Erin's recipes have appeared in numerous publications, including *Good Morning America Cut the Calories Cookbook* and Scottsdale, Arizona's KAET Channel 8 cookbook series, including *I is for International* and *E is for Entertaining*, SheSpeaks.com, Yahoo! Shine, *Where Women Cook* magazine, and *Experience Life* magazine.

Her first cookbook, *The Kitchen Pantry Cookbook*, was an Amazon bestseller and was nominated for the IACP (International Association of Culinary Professionals) Julia Child Best First Cookbook Award.

Erin is a frequent presenter at conferences and seminars around the world, discussing topics ranging from food photography to culinary trends and recipe development.

She has also appeared on numerous television and radio programs to demonstrate recipes and talk food. In October 2014, she appeared on, and won, Food Network's *Guy's Grocery Games*, a cooking game show featuring professional chefs from across America.

Her great passion is teaching, having taught thousands of students over the past 20 years. She currently teaches throughout the Puget Sound area at PCC Natural Markets, Chefshop.com, The Book Larder, Blue Ribbon Cooking and Culinary Center, The Chef's Kitchen, and privately through her own company, The Glorified HomeChef.